KNOWING, DOING, AND BEING

New Foundations for
Consciousness Studies

CHRIS CLARKE

imprint-academic.com

Copyright © Chris Clarke, 2013

The moral rights of the author have been asserted.
No part of this publication may be reproduced in any form
without permission, except for the quotation of brief passages
in criticism and discussion.

Published in the UK by
Imprint Academic, PO Box 200, Exeter EX5 5YX, UK

Distributed in the USA by
Ingram Book Company,
One Ingram Blvd., La Vergne, TN 37086, USA

ISBN 9781845404550

A CIP catalogue record for this book is available from the
British Library and US Library of Congress

Contents

Introduction	1
1. Defining Consciousness	4
1.1 The idea of consciousness	4
1.2 The origins of consciousness studies	5
1.3 The development of consciousness studies	8
1.4 Words	10
1.5 Self-consciousness	12
1.6 The seat of consciousness	14
1.7 Consciousness and the will	16
1.8 Subjective explorations of consciousness	18
2. Quantum	23
2.1 Interpreting Quantum theory	23
2.2 Certain uncertainty	27
2.3 What is quantum theory about?	29
2.4 But what about "The Field"?	34
2.5 Measurement and consciousness	36
2.6 Entanglement (spooky action at a distance)	40
2.7 Quantum theory today	42
2.8 Quantum cosmology	46
2.9 Histories: collapse without collapse	53
2.10 Selection in quantum cosmology	58
2.11 Between knowing and being	63
3. The Mind and its Logics: Knowing	67
3.1 The reinvention of knowing	67
3.2 The start of the separation: the language of duality	72
3.3 The rise of the propositional	77
3.4 Logic and mind	79
3.5 Truth and context	86

4. The Reinvention of Quantum Logic	92
4.1 Birkhoff-von Neumann logic	92
4.2 Context and degrees of truth	96
4.3 Superposition	98
5. What Does Consciousness Do?	101
5.1 Where the (quantum) buck stops	101
5.2 The operation of consciousness	103
5.3 Epiphenomenalism and the will	107
5.4 Models of the action of consciousness	112
5.5 Stapp's model	115
5.6 Orchestrated Objective Reduction	121
5.7 Assertion	123
5.8 The choice of nature	126
5.9 What does consciousness do to consciousness?	127
6. What Things Are Conscious?	131
6.1 Chasing consciousness	131
6.2 A propositional view of panpsychism	134
6.3 Things	135
6.4 The cosmos	139
7. A New Programme for Consciousness Research	145
7.1 The central aim	145
7.2 The pitfalls of the transliminal	148
7.3 Models of spirit	149
7.4 Praxis	151
7.5 Directions for the future	155
7.6 Wholeness	158
References	160
Endnotes	169

(**Note**: references like p. 32 refer to page numbers in the main text, while those like e. 80 refer to previously referenced endnote numbers.)

Introduction

Is there a connection between quantum theory and consciousness? There is a widespread feeling that, when it comes to basic principles, we do not understand either of these. They have mystery in common, so maybe they are somehow be connected! (A caricature, perhaps, of the response to this question.)

A more sophisticated response, which I take seriously, stems from the philosophy of Immanuel Kant: what we know about the world is conditioned by our capacity for knowing things, which establishes a connection at a fundamental level between knowing and what is known. Putting it very loosely indeed: when it comes to fundamentals, the basis of our knowing is consciousness, and so this will colour the basis of what is known.

My aim here is to explore this connection between quantum theory and consciousness. The exploration will disclose how we know about ourselves and the world, what we are, and how we act in the world—knowing, doing, and being.

Although most of this book concerns ideas and discoveries, their implications build a new story about our attitudes to the world and how we live in it, presented in the final chapter, which has practical consequences. I believe this new story is important for us and for our children: it is for lack of an inspiring, uplifting story that we are currently destroying ourselves and our planet.

Old stories, such as that "we are spiritual beings in a spiritual cosmos" may still at some level be true, but we can no longer relate to their language. Finding a new language will, in this book, take us on a long journey: to the earliest moments in the cosmos and back again. And for our equipment in travelling we will need the latest findings in cosmology, quantum physics, and psychology, along with more established ideas from philosophy.

My central concept will be "consciousness" — perhaps the most confusing term in academic discourse. Practically everyone who uses the term means something different. As the book proceeds I will be honing down this word into a concept that matches our need to understand the universe; but as a starting point I will be using it to refer to the essentially subjective aspect of our knowing, as distinct from the more formal part of our knowing that we can explicitly share with others through language.

One undercurrent flowing through the book is the idea (going back, in a different form, to the twelfth-century Hugh of St Victor) that most of the time we look at the world through one (metaphorical) "eye". The modern version, based on recent research, is that our minds have multiple components, many of which we neglect. In the version I will be using, I will refer to the two most important components of the mind as the *relational* and the *propositional*, and will argue that both must be fully taken into account if we are to understand the universe as a whole. The dominant scientific view rests only on our propositional knowing but nonetheless it identifies our current scientific theories with "reality". Here we will be seeking a wholeness of knowing greater than this.

While physicists investigating fundamental particles give the impression that the last details of our understanding are now being tidied up and completed, in reality it seems as though we are only just starting to approach the real challenge: that of integrating the physical with the spiritual.

The structure of this book inevitably reflects this fragmented state of our knowing, while at the same time endeavouring to heal it. The flow of the argument is given in the opening and closing notes to each chapter, while the sections between these present a series of interconnected topics drawing on consciousness studies, philosophy, spiritual teaching, and mathematical physics (quantum theory and quantum cosmology). While I have made my presentation of these subjects non-technical, as far as is possible, many of them will be more comprehensible to some readers than to others; so I have ensured that the thread of my argument will not be lost by the reader's skipping some of the sections. Where possible, detailed deductions, quotes from original sources, and less important amplifications are in the endnotes.

This is a field where the "easy" (but often challenging) work has been done, only to open to view, as when gaining the crest of a mountain ridge, a new uncharted territory still unexplored. Many of its features became clearer in the course of writing this book. So the reader will find many signposts to the unknown, as much as solutions to old riddles.

NB. References like p. 32 refer to page numbers in the main text, while those like e. 80 refer to previously referenced endnote numbers.

One

Defining Consciousness

Everything that we know depends on consciousness: without it there would be no I and so no we; without it there would be no knowing and so no known world. And yet "consciousness" is hard to define. Different authors use the word in different ways and so they say different things about it. Confusion is rife. In this chapter I explain how the various concepts to do with consciousness have changed over time; I compare the different meanings of the word as used historically and by recent authors; and I clarify what I am going to mean by the word in this book. I also map out some of the main ideas that have emerged from different traditions within the study of consciousness.

1.1 The idea of consciousness

The word "consciousness" is an abstraction, attempting to grasp at the reality of being human. That reality is our world, which we build up through a succession of experiences. As we develop through childhood this swirling, buzzing world takes on progressively more shape, containing *things*: people, animals, trees... And the world contains "Me", and all the distinct activities that I recognise, such as sleeping, waking, talking, inner talking... the ground of humanness on which we can build lives that can be creative and fulfilling.

There is an activity about this knowing; it is not just a stream flowing over us, but we are involved. Sometimes we *notice* things in a distinct succession — the sound of the wind in the trees, the scent of roses — and sometimes we may be focussed away from these particular things and we are unconscious of them. There are the radical shifts of our sleep and our dreaming. And then our curiosity starts asking "why" about all this structure. We might wonder, for instance, if there is a mental device that turns on and off our noticing. So we are starting to invent "consciousness".

The basic thread running through this book is a rethinking of the nature of the world. But weaving a counterpoint around this thread like a labyrinth is the idea of consciousness. The trouble with "consciousness" is that it has many meanings and most of them are subtle and intangible. The study of consciousness, however, embraces so many vitally important ideas that we need to survey it at the outset.

1.2 The origins of consciousness studies

Intellectual theories as to how our awareness works (in whole or in part) have abounded at least from Democritus (fl. 400 BCE) with ideas about how vision worked (see Park, 1997), to the present day. Alongside proto-scientific approaches like that of Democritus there were many traditional ways of visualising the human person as made up of several components: in the West, these were body, soul, and spirit. This strand of Western ideas reached its climax in 1637 with Descartes' very detailed theory of how human beings worked. He carried out many careful dissections of (often rather mangled) animal and human bodies, and came to the conclusion that the body worked rather like the pneumatically controlled moving puppets popular in Descartes' time, with "spirits" flowing down the nerves from the brain to the muscles which they activated into movement.

On this basis, Descartes saw human life as a two-component process in which activity was divided up between a mechanical body combined with a non-material soul. The body processed data from the senses of smelling, seeing, pain, and so on; it transmitted these into the third ventricle, a fluid-filled cavity in the brain; the soul then homed in on this combined data set, experienced it, and decided on any appropriate action; the soul then finally moved the pineal gland (which Descartes erroneously thought was inside the third ventricle) so as to direct the activating "spirits" into the right nerves so as to generate the appropriate movements of the body.

Considering the primitive state of science at that time, this was in essence a remarkable achievement. The anatomical details were revised and improved in due course, but the fundamental weakness of the approach remained untouched: all the difficult aspects—consciousness, will, the sense of self, language—were bundled together into the "soul" which was supposed to take care of them as if by magic. Descartes' legacy was to hang over philosophy and consciousness studies for the next three centuries.

The concept in Descartes' work that is closest to our present idea of consciousness is "apperception" (Descartes, 1649). This was a particular sort of perception involving not only the body receiving information through the senses, but also the soul in an act of will, or of paying attention. Later writers retained this term, but placed less reliance on the split between soul and body. Leibniz (1714), for example, wrote that "the passing state... is what is called perception. This must be distinguished from apperception, or conscious awareness."

The term "apperception" then comes into its own with Kant, whose basic approach (though not the copious details) has had a strong influence on this book. For him, the core activity of the human being is the interplay between, on the one hand, sense-perception (what we get immediately from our senses) and, on the other hand, our *understanding* of sense-perception in relation to ourselves. Sense-perception and understanding form a duality, related to each other as object and subject, respectively. Kant calls the basis of understanding "apperception".

A crucial part of Kant's scheme presented in his *Critique of Pure Reason* is the idea that we do not have a hotline to reality. The world in itself, what Kant called the *noumenon,* is unknowable and all we have are its "representations" — items conveyed by the senses and grasped by understanding. Though the duality introduced by Descartes remains, in the hands of Kant both components can be, and are, investigated in great detail. Natural Philosophy (science) can investigate what is delivered to us through perception and the philosophy of mind can investigate apperception. What we regard as "the world" is composed from the two. This is an approach that will be pursued in much of this book: the world as we receive it and live it is to be understood through a dual analysis of both what is internal to human understanding and what we receive from external existence.

Kant's conclusion on analysing this situation[1] is that perception (from the senses) and apperception (from understanding) each display an "original unity". The unity of perception is the structure of space and time. The unity of apperception is bound up with the sense of "me"; without this our apperceptions "would not be grasped together in a self-consciousness". Another way in which he puts this is that this unity is "something under which every intuition must stand in order to become an object for me" otherwise "the manifold would not be united in one consciousness".[2] We can note here the use of most of the key terms in consciousness studies: the use of the word "consciousness" (Bewußtsein); the role of the self, "me"; and the issue of unity which will be taken up in detail later in this book (§6.3[p. 135]).

To summarise, from Kant's analysis I will be drawing on three points:
1. We have no hotline to reality; all we have are our perceptions and their incorporation in our understanding.

We can, however, continually enlarge perception and understanding through science and kindred disciplines.
2. Our apperceptions do not in themselves define or give rise to the unity that we are aware of; rather, this unity has to be in some way a fundamental (*"a priori"*) part of the process of apperception.
3. Apperception, with its essential unity, seems to be linked with a sense of "me" and from this viewpoint is called "self-consciousness" (this will be clarified later, §1.5p. 12).

1.3 The development of consciousness studies

If we now jump forward to the modern world, we find a very different intellectual framework. The dominant world-view is that of scientific realism, in which the structure that is being progressively revealed by science is the foundation for all that is, including our own personal existence. The power of the scientific method rests on its objectivity, the insistence that every piece of evidence must be replicable by any appropriately equipped observer, and that the process of observation must itself be public: the scientist is only allowed to rely on data or procedures which are capable of being observed publicly and replicated independently.

The data of consciousness, on the other hand, is by its nature personal: it is what *I* am experiencing, and while an observer can monitor my neural activity they cannot, it would seem, share what this is like for me.

There have been two entirely opposed philosophical reactions to this current situation. The first (Dennett, 1991) holds that the parts of Descartes' picture that are concerned with the soul are redundant; that we already have in our modern mechanistic picture of the body an essentially adequate account of the nature of the human being—though of course many details remain to be filled in—and no other extra fundamental features or entities need to be added. The thing that is given the special name "consciousness" is just the moment-by-moment way in which the brain links together sounds, scents, inner talking, and so on in a constantly changing series of "drafts": organized relationships between bits of sensory data and bits of memory that help us navigate in the world.

The second reaction to the modern intellectual situation claims that the mechanistic picture entirely misses out the most important aspect of humans, from the human point of view, namely my subjective experience of *what it is like to be me,* at each given moment. This is what I am, my very being. The mechanistic approach can only explain what I *do*, observed from the outside; but this "what it is like to be me" is necessarily observed from the inside. It is subjective rather than objective. To bring home this essentially subjective sense of consciousness, Nagel (1974) considered the starker problem of imagining what it might be like to be a bat, arguing that the best I could ever manage is what it would be like *for me to be a bat*; whereas the question is, what is it like *for a bat to be a bat*. We could get a complete account of how the bat was linking up its sensory data (different though they are from ours) but that does not get us the slightest bit nearer to understanding what this is like for the bat. This demonstrates, he claimed, the essential subjectivity of being a bat, from which we can, correspondingly, understand the essential subjectivity of being me.

The introduction of a private, non-verbal, and subjective element that is essential for understanding consciousness is a dramatic step going beyond both Kant's approach (which was based on publicly sharable verbal analysis) and Dennett's approach. We will see later in chapter 4 why it is, from a psychological point of view, that there are two such diametrically opposed views, represented by Dennett and Nagel.

Later David Chalmers (1995) supported Nagel's argument and stressed the difficulty of the task ahead of us in trying to grasp and understand our subjective experience. He called this, with ironic understatement, "the hard problem of consciousness studies".

1.4 Words

The entry in the *Oxford English Dictionary* for "consciousness" runs to 3300 words,[3] reflecting the many different nuances of the word. A simpler word for what we are concerned with here is "awareness". When I am awake or dreaming I am aware, whereas in deep sleep or a coma I am not (Velmans, 2000, p. 6). "Awareness" also carries the sense of subjectivity present in Chalmers' usage of "consciousness". But the word "consciousness" is entrenched in the discipline of consciousness studies, the main focus of this book, and so I will be using the word in the sense of subjective awareness as just explained. More precisely, by "consciousness" I will mean the phenomenon, faculty, or process in which a person has awareness in the present moment, and which constitutes what it is like being that person at that moment. That is to say, I will be using the word in the sense in which it is understood (or, for others, "misunderstood") by Nagel and Chalmers, namely as the form of our total subjective experience.

Another word that often comes up in this context is "qualia" — the plural of "quale", from Latin, meaning property or quality. It is supposed to refer to *how* a thing is rather than *what* it is. The snag with this term is that it doesn't go far enough. Certainly particular subjective qualia such as the scent of a rose are a part of consciousness; but perhaps the most interesting thing about consciousness is the way that these qualia are brought together into a subjective whole, into the totality of my conscious experience at some particular moment. The question of how this occurs is called "the binding problem", which we can recognise as precisely the aspect of "unity" that played such a crucial role in Kant's analysis. As Revonsuo (1999) expressed it, somehow "[t]he contents of phenomenal consciousness are unified into one coherent whole, containing a unified 'me' in the center of one unified perceptual world, full of coherent objects."

Revonsuo points out that there are at least two aspects to the binding problem: there is the neurological aspect of how the many scattered neural processes that correspond to, say, our experience of a rose (its scent, its visual appearance, evoked items of memory...) are connected together in the wiring of the brain; and there is the experiential, subjective one of what it is about our experience that makes not only the rose, but all the things that we are perceiving cohere into a whole.[4]

Perhaps the most interesting aspect of this is the introduction of "me" into the concept of unified experience, as was the case with Kant. Not only is this a possible source of the unity of consciousness, but also, in view of the considerations of Nagel, could this "me" be the source of the subjectivity of consciousness? In the language of qualia, do individual qualia acquire their subjective character from an internal "me"; or is the subjective nature of "me" constructed from the subjectivity of various qualia that make up the "me"?

Even more importantly, what is this fundamental but illusive concept of "me" or "self"? Is the self just a name for a bundle of sensation, or is there an independent entity of some sort whose operation performs the bundling? While even the simplest animals must have some binding mechanism for producing a coherent action out of stimuli that are recorded in many different parts of the brain, is there a sense of "self" that is unique to humans, and is it "self-consciousness", in the sense of an awareness that includes an aspect of the "self", that we really refer to when we talk about "consciousness"? And might this mean that Descartes, with his notion of the "soul", was right all along?

1.5 Self-consciousness

It might be helpful at this stage to list the questions or hypotheses about the self/me/'I' that are raised by the ideas introduced so far.

1. Does talk about the "self" refer ambiguously to many different concepts, or is there one central concept with possible variants?
2. (The chicken-or-egg question) Which of these is the case:
   a. Each conscious being is associated with an entity, traditionally called a soul, which creates the *unity* of apperception introduced by Kant, solves thereby the binding problem, and in addition imparts the ineffable subjectivity of conscious experience argued by Nagel and expressed in the notion of qualia. Or,
   b. Each moment and each component of consciousness has its own quale, and in addition there exists a natural process that brings these together into an enduring unity, which we then call a self.
3. How does the self relate to different forms of thinking,[5] including thinking-about-my-thoughts (reflexive thinking)?
4. Is the self a fundamental structure present in a human from the start, or does it progressively develop?

It is clear that the answer to 1 is that "self" means many things. One of the most usual senses is of "me" as a social concept that I think about. How did *I* manage that task? What is she thinking about *me*? This need not be verbal: it can be a sense of my own worth or worthlessness which shapes my decisions, or a sense of my place (either literally or metaphorically) in relation to others around me. "I" am a person and we build up concepts of what this person is like, as well as experiencing snapshots of what "I" am doing and how it is to be "me". The Self as an object within consciousness is widely regarded as a construction, developed throughout life (Backhurst &

Sypnowich, 1995; Harter, 2001) — answering question 4 above in this particular sense of self as a social construct. This sense is relevant to self-consciousness in the sense of "I always feel very self-conscious when I am with them." I will be saying more about this in Chapter 3,[p. 70] when it will become clearer that the form in which we experience self-consciousness is probably based on a distinctively human organisation of the brain.

This sense, however, is quite different from the deeper "self consciousness" as the term is used by Kant, referring simply to the wholeness that arises from the unity of our thoughts. It is not a construct that is progressively developed, but is a basic condition associated with any sort of apperception or thinking.

Another more specialised aspect of human consciousness is the fact the we can think *about* what we are perceiving at the same time as experiencing it. Our consciousness can be turning back on itself in order to think about thinking, becoming reflexive in the sense of "reflecting upon" the current stream of awareness.[e. 5] It could be a matter of thinking about perceptions, whether of external objects or internal bodily states, or of *reflecting* on memory — either on a memory recalled from the past or on part of the continuous stream of short-term memory that gives coherence to our consciousness. In what follows, and in distinction to Kant, I shall use the term "self-consciousness" to refer to this reflexive consciousness, and "subjective consciousness" or simply "consciousness" to refer to the qualitative "what it is like" associated with the unified apperceptions described by Kant, a unity which warrants the term "me", but only as a label for this unity, not as a structure in its own right.

To return briefly to what I am calling self-consciousness, however: this notion does give one a handle on a form of consciousness that one might identify in creatures other than the human. Though it is not easy to decide whether or not higher animals have some sort of self-consciousness, there does seem to be solid evidence for reflexivity in higher primates (de Veer & Van den Bos, 1999) and some cetaceans (L. Marino, 2002). When, however, it comes to consciousness in the more general sense being used here, we barely know how to begin to draw any line between humans and other organisms.

A major theme in this book will centre on this question of what things/beings are conscious and where to draw the line. Nagel was assuming that there was something that it was like to be a bat, even though we could never know what it was, and therefore that bats were in some sense conscious. Our basic concept of consciousness is human consciousness, and the further we get from human beings the more reluctant we become to acknowledge that they, in however primitive a sense, possess the basic essentials of what we think of as our consciousness — whatever that may be. We will need to fill out our notion of consciousness further before we can address this issue properly.

1.6 The seat of consciousness

As well as the "what" of consciousness there is a related "where" of consciousness. An important and interesting sense of this arises from the philosophical question of whether, from a proper subjective view, my consciousness has a "where". Certainly many of the things that I am conscious *of* have a place: certainly visually received things, but very often also sounds and bodily senses such as textures that are touched, itches, and so on — these occupy places in a sort of subjective "space"; and the question then arises as to how this relates to physical space (Alexander, 1920; Velmans, 2000). In this case I could imagine my consciousness as extending out to embrace these textures, etc. so that my consciousness was a sort of octopus extending from my body; but this would seem to most Western people a rather gratuitous construction. I say "I am consciousness" and I associate "I" with my whole body, but I do not have a sense of my consciousness *occupying* my body in the way that, say, my blood does. It would seem that my consciousness belongs to the category of things that do not properly have physical places, just as, say, verbs do not have a physical place.

While asking for a "where" of consciousness does not seem helpful, it does make sense to ask for the "where" of whatever it is that underlies and produces consciousness. In Descartes' theory, for example, consciousness was a product of the soul, which does not have a "where", but it is supposed to interact with the body by being present to the third ventricle of the brain, and especially to the pineal gland (which he erroneously thought was inside this ventricle). This sort of "where" is usually called the *seat* of consciousness. In modern theories it might be various other parts of the brain. Where one looks for this location depends very much on the sort of theory being used. On a traditional neurological approach one will be looking for particular configurations of neurons. With the rise of quantum mechanical explanations of consciousness, however, authors focus on much more fine-scale structures, such as neurotransmitter receptors (Stapp, 2007)[p. 115] or even tiny structures inside individual cells (Hameroff & Penrose, 1996). The more the physical foundations of consciousness are divided into fragments, the harder it becomes to account for the subjective feeling that consciousness is a single integrated whole. This physical foundation resembles not so much a "seat" as a scattering of white stones amongst a beach of black ones.

There is, however, a countervailing argument to this, to do with the possibly illusory nature of the single undivided "I". Teasdale and Barnard (1993), to whom we will return in section 3.1,[p. 67] have argued that our mind is best understood as constituted by at least nine semi-autonomous subsystems, of which only two contribute explicitly to the conscious self. If I reflect on my own awareness, I often find decisions arising from a strand of feeling (Teasdale and Barnard's "implicational subsystem", called "relational" here) which I had been ignoring until it made its presence more strongly felt, and in meditation, when the dominant verbal component (Teasdale and Barnard's "propositional subsystem") is momentarily silenced, I can note other more subtle processes taking place of which I was unaware.

This multiple model can be further expanded into the thesis of Lockwood (1989) that we have a "compound I" constituted from many elements. As I shall argue in section 5.5, there is evidence that quantum processes in the brain can have a hierarchical structure, in which processes at the microscopic level, having the nature of consciousness but way below personal awareness, contribute to a chain of increasingly larger structures, up to the "I" of traditional philosophy.

1.7 Consciousness and the will

The sensations that make up our subjective experience, "what is like to be me", include many mental activities in addition to experiencing impressions from our senses and reflections on these. As Descartes (Meditation ii) puts it:

> But what, then, am I? A thinking thing, it has been said. But what is a thinking thing? It is a thing that doubts, understands, [conceives],[6] affirms, denies, wills, refuses; that imagines also, and perceives. (Descartes, 1641 [Veitch, 1901])

One of the most interesting items in this list is "wills": we are aware of deciding things and then carrying out our decision. The carrying out is not so mysterious: in itself, carrying out a plan already formulated is something that computers can, and do, achieve, very often more efficiently than we do. "Deciding", however, is different. It is the performing of a shift from surveying a range of possibilities presented within a particular subjective context to affirming a particular direction within what is usually a shifted subjective context. And in practice there is a period of time in which deciding and considering the carrying out proceed together. This is the process of willing. Just as sensations like the fleeting scent of a rose seem to be an integral part of my consciousness, so also do acts of will. It seems to us that we have the capacity not only to contemplate things, but to cause things — in the first place causing actions of our own body, but as a result causing wider consequences in the world.

Both perceiving and willing have an essentially subjective nature. In expounding what I subjectively feel *and what I subjectively will* to another person, the best I can do is to evoke in her what these processes would be like for her, on the presumption that this is similar to what it is like for me. Thus within "consciousness" I will include willing.[7] This means that consciousness does things. There is a two-way interaction between the larger world and myself, in which my perceptions are caused by the world and my internal conscious processes cause things to happen in the world.

Note that a concept quite close to "will" is "responsibility", as in the phrase "I am responsible for my own actions". There are, however, some subtle distinctions between the two. In a general sense, "will" is to do with autonomy: acting as an initiating cause of an action as opposed to being just a cog in a wheel. Responsibility goes further than this, however, because it implies that I have to some extent reflected on my action. It is linked, in other words, with the self. If a person in a trial is acquitted of being guilty of a crime by reason of "diminished responsibility", this does not mean that he did not will it (as might have been the case if it was an accident) but that he did not connect the act with the moral and social elements that constitute the self. As with the self, I will mostly not be dealing with responsibility in this book.

1.8 Subjective explorations of consciousness

The most systematic and extensive examination of consciousness has taken place within the spiritual traditions; indeed, "working with consciousness" might almost be the definition of spirituality. There are, however, obvious problems with connecting philosophical enquiry and spiritual practice, to say nothing of mutual suspicion between those involved. Usually the aim of philosophy is logical understanding while that of spirituality is internal liberation, and these may not be compatible. From a pejorative perspective one might suspect that spiritual practices are not investigating consciousness but distorting it and then putting a doctrinally motivated gloss on the result.

An open-minded approach to consciousness seems clearest in the Madhyamaka and Dzogchen Buddhist traditions, where there is strong emphasis on simply paying attention to consciousness and not imposing any external image upon it. The Buddhist writer Alan Wallace (who also holds a physics degree) describes how one can "so profoundly settle the mind that virtually all thoughts and other mental constructs become dormant". Eventually "the culmination of this meditative process is the experience of the *substrate consciousness* (*ālaya-vijñāna*), which is characterized by three essential traits: bliss, luminosity and non-conceptuality" (Wallace, 2007, p. 45). In the Dzogchen tradition this consciousness is called *rigpa*. Sogyal Rinpoche (2002, p. 158) quotes Patrul Rinpoche, that "the nature of mind, the face of Rigpa, is introduced upon the very dissolution of the conceptual mind."

What is claimed here, based on experiences that seem clear even for a beginner in a mediation technique, is that the basic ground of consciousness is the reverse of the nature that many neurologically inclined philosophers attach to it. For the latter, consciousness is merely a linking-together of many different processes handling percepts, reflections, etc. For the meditator, consciousness is what supports the existence of these percepts: it is progressively revealed as an independent realm as the percepts settle down and cease attracting our attention.

The theistic religions mainly use a different language, phrasing their experiences in terms of a relationship with God in a way which often seems to distort the picture. For many authors, however, their conclusions are nonetheless comparable to those just quoted from Buddhism. Meister Eckhart gives us glimpses of his experience, using language as best he can (and certainly not consistently) to point to what is non-conceptual, a realm that implicitly includes consciousness. For example, he makes a distinction between the God of scripture and God in the sense of "the Godhead" which is entirely beyond concepts, praying "that God may rid [him] of 'God'". Then within this context he describes how "God must become utterly I, and I utterly God, so fully one that this 'he' and this 'I' become and are *one* 'essential is', and in this essence eternally work *one* work"[8] (Quint, 1955, Pr83: DIII, 47, 5f). Modern Christian theologians tend to interpret this "work" as the Father's begetting of the Son, but though this is included in the concept, it is clear from Eckhart's writings that the "work" is Being, from which creativity "boils over", with the emergence of the Son as part of this fecundity. Thus the experiences he is describing are ones where his individuality becomes included in pure Being. We might say of this that "his" consciousness becomes included in a universal consciousness, or we might say it becomes apparent that consciousness in itself is universal.

In both the Christian and the Buddhist accounts there is ambiguity as to whether the state of consciousness that is disclosed in such experiences is "my" consciousness or "universal" Consciousness. Or, to put it more accurately, since this state is beyond all mental constructs, these becoming "dormant", the labels of "mine" or "God's" cannot be attached to it.[9] This is interesting in connection with the ideas of Kant which we have just examined. At first glance we might suppose that Kant's insistence that we cannot know absolute reality, the *noumenon*, was at odds with Eckhart's claim about becoming "utterly God". But these are reconciled through the distinction between knowing and being. Eckhart is not claiming to know God, but to share the being-ness of God.

This distinction is related to one that I will be discussing in section 3.1[p. 67] between propositional and relational (or "implicational") knowing, developed through extensive research at the MRC Cognition and Brain Sciences Unit in Cambridge by John Teasdale and Philip Barnard. *Relational knowing* is sharing the being of another person or thing, whereas *propositional knowing* is grasping a thing with rational analysis. These two ways operate through two distinct "cognitive subsystems" in the brain. Consciousness, as I am considering it in this book, in fact underpins both of these, whereas Kant's accounts tend to focus on the propositional aspect of it.

One interpretation of investigations such as these is the idea that consciousness is, in its essence, *simple*. Much of the time the content of our experience is hugely complex, and the apparatus of the brain that generates this content, as well as generating a panoply of other happenings untouched by consciousness, is vastly more complex. But the witness of those who put aside what is *in* consciousness in order to be alone with being points not to complexity but to the simplicity of oneness.

This brief dip into spirituality turns up a number of vital ideas. They will be explored at length in the chapters to follow, but here are some preliminary headlines regarding what is suggested by this sort of subjective experience:

1. Subjective exploration reveals aspects of consciousness which are not merely less precise, but are fundamentally different from those disclosed by philosophical and physical analysis. Since consciousness is by definition subjective, this suggests that subjective

exploration is an essential part of investigating consciousness, yielding information that is more relevant than that from analysis.
2. When investigated subjectively, consciousness seems to be a thing in itself that supports percepts, rather than a thing constructed out of percepts.
3. There does not seem to be a clear line between consciousness that is localised to one person and consciousness that seems more universal. (It seems, from a strictly logical perspective, paradoxical that something that by its definition is fundamentally personal and incommunicable can at the same time be universal.)

If the deeper aspects of consciousness that appear from introspection were no more than an additional gloss on the materialistic treatment of consciousness, a gloss that only appeared during practices associated with spirituality, then they could be dismissed as a possibly illusory appearance that had no direct relevance to a systematic theory based on public evidence and correlation with neurological data. I will argue later, however, for a second reason why we cannot dismiss the subjective view of consciousness in favour of scientific rationality; namely, because aspects of quantum theory are dependent on the nature of consciousness, in a way that supports the view from spiritual traditions. This remains the case despite several recent attempts to find alternatives to this conclusion. If this is indeed the case, then consciousness can only be understood through a combination of subjective and objective investigations, with due regard being taken of the very different natures of these two approaches.

Such a joint approach takes us into very new areas of thought, indeed into a radical view of the nature of the world around us. In the next chapter I will survey this unfamiliar landscape, in preparation for a more detailed analysis of its various aspects.

Synopsis

- Following Kant, we note that
  a. "The world" is as much a product of our particular ways of knowing as it is of the cosmos
  b. Our knowledge of reality is composed from "perception" (the input from the senses) and "apperception" (its reception in the individual self)
  c. Apperception does not refer to the "me" which is a construction, but to a fundamental unity that is the ground of consciousness.
- Consciousness expresses "what it is like to be..."
- Consciousness itself does not have a "place", but there may be a physically located "seat of consciousness" interfacing with thinking and perceiving.
- Consciousness may be "compound" — arising from smaller sub-consciousnesses while still manifesting a unity in itself. Manifestations of this may be
  a. the division into cognitive subsystems of Teasdale and Barnard (here named "propositional" and "relational");
  b. the inclusion of our consciousness in a greater one, suggested by spiritual exploration.
- Spiritual concepts and techniques have an important role in subjective exploration by virtue of their access to the relational subsystem. This exploration suggests an aspect of consciousness that is global rather than individual.
- Willing is part of consciousness.

Two

Quantum

My basic thesis – which many would dispute – is that there is a strong connection between consciousness and quantum theory. Quantum theory reveals what consciousness is, while consciousness plays an active role in the operation of quantum physics. However, just as there are many senses of the word "consciousness" so there are many expressions and interpretations of quantum theory. This chapter explains the basic ideas of quantum theory, the varieties of different formulations of the subject, and its connections (according to some of these formulations) with consciousness.

2.1 Interpreting quantum theory[10]

The title of this section should seem odd. These days, we rarely discuss a problem with "interpreting botany" or "interpreting geology": crudely speaking, botany is about plants and geology is about the material structure of the earth. But when it comes to quantum theory, although we have a clear and systematic picture expounded in many textbooks on how to carry out quantum mechanical calculations in a variety of different settings, the question is still often raised, "what is it really *about*?" And very often the answer is "it depends on which interpretation you take". It also depends on what you mean by "really". As with consciousness studies in the last chapter, a brief historical sketch may be helpful, this time focusing on the changing relationships between science and reality.

"Reality" is a term usually opposed to "illusion", "simulation", or "falsehood". Once the illusion is broken, the simulation found wanting or the falsehood exposed, then the metaphorical scales fall from our eyes and we discern reality. This concept is dominant with Plato, who likened the illusory nature of our common, unreflective concept of the world to a mere moving shadow of reality; and also in Eastern religions where the human state prior to enlightenment is an immersion in "maya" (illusion). This idea is also implicitly present in classical physics where Newton's picture of atoms moving according to precise laws in the void is the reality that underlies the pretty and unpredictable phenomena created by our senses. And it is there in Crick's assertion (1994) that we human beings are "nothing but a pack of neurons", echoing the discovery by Alice in *Alice in Wonderland* that what she had previously taken for people were "nothing but a pack of playing cards". While scientists often regard their goal as the uncovering of reality, post-enlightenment philosophers are usually more cautious. We have seen, for example, how Kant denies the possibility of knowing a thing *in itself*, or knowing its reality *for itself*.[11]

The trouble with "reality" is that it is too comprehensive a concept to be philosophically useful: it encompasses both the fact *that* something is (its existence) and *what* something is (its form). These two aspects, being and form, belong to the two different forms of knowing examined in section 1.6: I perceive the concrete presence of a person or object through an immediate non-verbal encounter, engaging my relational subsystem; then as I figure out what sort of a person or thing this is in front of me I bring in, in addition, my propositional subsystem. Because of the separation of these two subsystems in modern Western culture, that is documented by McGilchrist (2009; see §3.1[p. 67]), it is not surprising that it is hard to bring being and form together into a viable notion of reality. Yet we do need to bring them together if we are to form a rounded awareness of our world, even if it would still be exaggerated to call the result "reality".

To return now to quantum theory, with its competing "interpretations", it is useful to examine the way in which it progressively broke free from the grandiose belief of classical physics that it had reality within its grasp, and entered a period where some scientists were more cautious, recognising that the nature of the world was more subtle than had been supposed in the triumphalist period following Newton.

In the formative early work on quantum theory in the 1920s, the theory was "about" laboratory experiments on microscopic "systems" — that is, on particular objects or collections of objects that had been artificially selected for investigation in a laboratory experiment. Although these might hold little practical interest in everyday life, there was a universal scientific belief that the universe as a whole was simply an aggregate of such laboratory systems, and that all large-scale events could "in principle" be deduced from a knowledge of small-scale ones. This was "reality"!

To take a simple case, when Galileo measured the acceleration under gravity of balls rolling down an incline, there was an implicit possibility that one could extrapolate from rolling balls to fired cannonballs and thence to the solar system (even though such an extrapolation might not be entirely straightforward).[12] Such a belief had driven science, with great success, from the time of Newton onwards. It was a belief that the physical universe (whatever one might add on in the way of spiritual components) was real and mechanical: at each moment there was a definite "the way things are" and immutable laws governed the way things change from moment to moment (again, with spiritual influences as optional extras).

Quantum theory, however, seemed somewhat different, in that there were strict limits on how much information one could gather in any one experiment, limits set down by what came to be known as the uncertainty principle,[13] developed by Werner Heisenberg in 1927. According to this principle, for each system there was a basic catalogue of measurements that it was possible to make with controllable results (though none could be made with complete accuracy). Moreover, for each measurement there was a particular second measurement, called the "complementary" measurement to the first, such that the more accurately you carried out the first measurement the less accurately you could perform the second. If there was a reality here, it seemed to be a reality that hid itself.[14] At the pivotal Solvay conference of 1927, Albert Einstein and Neils Bohr fiercely debated the reality that might lie behind quantum theory. Einstein insisted that "There exists an element of physical reality" (Einstein *et al.*, 1935, p. 777), while Bohr was to conclude that "There is no quantum world" (Petersen, 1963). For each hypothetical experiment devised by Einstein to reveal the face of reality, Bohr was able to show that reality, if it existed, was in fact hidden: that the uncertainty principle still held. The debate rumbled on among many other protagonists until it was finally clinched by Kochen and Specker (1967) who showed that for any system more complex than a single electron at rest in empty space it was actually *logically impossible for the system to have* exact values for all possible measurements, irrespective of whether or not one could measure them.[15] So uncertainty was not a consequence of the clumsiness of physicists' apparatus, but something built into the very structure of existence. There might be "a quantum world" — but it would be not as we know it. In particular, as Kochen and Specker showed very explicitly, there was something peculiar about the logic of any quantum world. This aspect of logic will be a recurring theme for us.

2.2 Certain uncertainty

Uncertainty plays a major role in quantum theory. This contrasts with classical physics which is, in a sense, certain but is rendered uncertain in circumstances where we have incomplete information. Quantum theory, on the other hand, is fundamentally uncertain and there is no missing information that would render it certain. Its uncertainty is forced by the logic of the Kochen-Specker theorem and not by human frailty. It is tempting to think that this is the only real difference between classical and quantum physics, and the work of Prigogine (1997) does indeed suggest that the difference between them is not as great as was thought. Part of the importance of the Kochen-Specker theorem, however, is its demonstration that there are some sorts of uncertainty that are inevitable: we can be certain about this quantum uncertainty — or "certain uncertainty". It is, moreover, particularly significant when considering the role of consciousness in quantum theory.

In many situations there is an interplay between the uncertainty of quantum theory and the uncertainty that we are more familiar with, and it will be helpful to understand the difference between the two before considering further the nature of quantum theory.

As an example of quantum uncertainty, let us consider a seminal experiment regarding the logical principles of quantum theory (Gerlach & Stern, 1922). Otto Stern and Walther Gerlach set up an experiment in which a stream of silver atoms having a natural magnetic polarity, like tiny bar-magnets, was projected through a vacuum chamber. There they passed between the two facing poles of a shaped magnet and each atom was deflected towards one or other of the poles. In classical physics this would normally be regarded as an indication of the direction in which the polarity of the atom was pointing. The results were inconsistent with a conventional way of thinking about the situation, which today we would explain by attributing a *quantum state* to each atom. The quantum state influences the chances of the atom being deflected in one direction or another, while leaving some uncertainty as to which would actually take place. Importantly, once it is noted that a particular atom deflects towards, say, the North pole of the magnet, its quantum state is altered to a state which predicts the same result for any repeat testing of the particle in a second magnet placed further on and aligned in the same way as the first.

Consider now a different experiment involving classical "uncertain uncertainty", put forward as an objection to quantum theory by the philosopher of science Karl Popper.[16] I toss a coin, cover it with my hand, and ask a friend to guess whether it is displaying heads or tails. The friend is uncertain because she does not have enough information. I then reveal which is the case. We could assign a "quantum state" to the coin when it is covered, which gives probabilities of 1/2 to each of head and tails; and we could declare that when my friend looked at the coin this state collapsed into either a pure head state or a pure tail state (to use quantum terminology). This would, however, be regarded as a perverse way of describing it. Rather, we would say that actually the coin had a perfectly definite classical state all the time, either heads or tails, and the uncertainty lay not with the coin but with the information possessed by my friend. When further evidence is supplied, it is the information that changes, not the state of the coin.

The difference between the situation with the atoms and the situation with the coins is revealed by the Kochen-Specker theorem, which shows that, on logical grounds, there does not exist any catalogue of information that could consistently specify all behaviours of the atom under all directions in which a testing magnet might be oriented. The coin exhibits uncertain uncertainty: it all depends on how skilful my friend is at getting information, whether he peeked, and so on. The atom exhibits quantum uncertainty: the Kochen-Specker theorem fixes it rigorously and we know exactly how much of it there is, from the uncertainty relations.[e, 13]

In practice, the physicist or technologist is usually faced with a combination of the two uncertainties: the fact that some measurements must always have an intrinsic quantum mechanical effect associated with them, and also the fact that in practice not every aspect of an experimental situation can be specified with total accuracy, so that some relevant information will always be unavailable. The first is described in the formalism of quantum mechanics by the *quantum state* (dealt with in the next section) and the second one is described by a *probability distribution* in the formalism of probability theory.[17] When discussing general issues about measurement, as we will be doing shortly, it is convenient to combine these in a single entity called a *mixed state*.[18]

2.3 What is quantum theory about?

At this stage some fundamental ideas are needed in order to go any further. Specifically, I will describe the underlying context of quantum theory, the *quantum state* (touched on above), the *Hamiltonian* and *observables*. This will be followed by some remarks on "reality".

The context of quantum theory

To begin with, I will try to give an inkling of what a theoretical physicist does when examining a problem in quantum physics. First, one needs to get clear what sort of a *system* it is that one is studying. It might be an atom, or the nucleus of an atom interacting with a fast neutron coming towards it, or two particles interacting with each other, or a crystal of salt... Then, noting that simplifications have to be made in the problem if it is going to be at all tractable, one has to decide on a level of detail in the study that captures the essence of the system without getting bogged down in it. For example, in studying an atom the details of the nucleus can for many applications be ignored and the nucleus regarded as a blob carrying mass and charge. Or in studying a crystal, which is made up of a regular array of identical "cells" each built from a few atoms, one can focus on the physics of one cell together with general principles about how exactly a replicated pattern of cells can make up a macroscopic object.

While quantum theory is imbued with the ideas of laboratory experiments, there is nothing about it which sets a limit to how large the "laboratory" or the "system" might be. Later we will be considering the situation of quantum cosmology where the "system" is the entire universe and, since there is nothing bigger than the universe, the "laboratory" is itself. As we shall see, this creates an anomalous situation in which the conventional interpretations of physicists start to break down.

The quantum state and quantum space

Next — and this is the crux of quantum theory — one sets out the quantum mechanical description of the system that has been specified. The intuitive, essentially classical pictures that I have been referring to so far ("blobs", "coming towards") are represented by a mathematical structure, following procedures that have been found to work in the past. At an abstract level the core component of this structure is known as a "**quantum state**". It encapsulates all that can be known at a particular moment of time (some would say, all the properties that exist at that moment) as a result of the past history of that system. At a more concrete (but still mathematical) level suitable for practical computation it might be represented as what is metaphorically called a "wave" — or sometimes "wave function". Just as a real wave has a "value" consisting of a height and a speed that varies from point to point in the space beyond the beach where the wave is running, and just as a real wave changes with time, so this metaphorical wave has an abstract value (such as a collection of numbers) that varies with "points" in a generalisation of "space" and varies also with a purely numerical time. This sort of representation is the "wave function" championed by Schrödinger in the earliest days of quantum theory. An alternative but equivalent representation might be a collection of numbers (now called a "matrix") of the form championed by his rival, Werner Heisenberg.

Modern work, particularly at the very theoretical end, tends to work in terms of a mathematical "space", each point of which corresponds to an entire wave in Schrödinger's approach. This concentrates on the essential properties of a quantum state irrespective of how that state is represented. Here "space" is a term used for a sort of catalogue of mathematical objects (of which waves or matrices are examples) that share some particular mathematical property. The different objects are imagined as being systematically arranged beside each other so that their nature varies smoothly from one to a near neighbour. This whole arrangement of possible states is regarded as a "space" whose "points" are possible quantum states. I shall refer to a space of quantum states belonging to some particular system, whether it is a particle in a physics experiment or the entire universe, as a "quantum space",[e. 18] of which a space of wave functions or a space of matrices is a particular example.

The Hamiltonian and observables

In addition to a description of the system as a quantum state there needs to be an entity specifying the *dynamics* of the system: the rules that enforce just how the state changes with time. This entity is now called the **Hamiltonian**, in honour of William Hamilton who devised the version used for classical physics in the 1830s. It is the modern equivalent of Newton's laws of motion. Also procedures have to be specified that describe how the numerical properties of the system, the actual values of experimental measurements, are represented in the mathematics of the quantum state, procedures that involve a further type of mathematical structure called (somewhat ironically, in view of its abstract nature) an **observable**. This whole process of constructing the quantum state, the quantum Hamiltonian and the observables from their more visualisable versions in classical physics is called "quantisation". Once this is done, the physicist can start doing experiments and comparing the results with the predictions of the quantised mathematical model that she had devised.

Reality

In the context of this section the question is, where might "reality" be in all this? For my part, when I am developing mathematical models I feel that that mathematics, with its firm structures of logic and reasoning, is a sort of reality: albeit a reality that is cold and divorced from ordinary experience, but that has its own surprises and beauty. This is the sort of reality that Plato promoted, now often called "the Platonic world". For some physicists, once a particular theoretical quantum model has become well established and a way of thinking about it has become natural and intuitive, then that model itself becomes regarded as "reality" — at least as much so as either the old Newtonian picture or the often superficial view of things that we obtain from our unaided senses.

Roger Penrose (2004, p. 18, fig. 1.3) promotes a view of reality based on three interlocking realities: the Platonic mathematical world, the physical world, and the mental world. Each in turn gives rise to the next, with the mental world closing the loop by its creation of the Platonic world. This is within the spirit of this book, which rests on the idea of there being many different ways of knowing, each connecting together the two subsystems of our mind, the relational and the propositional, in a different way, and each opening a different window on an unbounded sea of being.[19]

By contrast, the Newtonian theory that ruled physics before quantum theory, increasingly coupled with a view of consciousness that regarded it as simply another physical phenomenon like heat or electricity, nurtured a hope that the probing of science into progressively more detailed constituents of matter would eventually reach the endpoint of the ultimate laws governing the entirety of existence. This approach lives on in the quest for the smallest constituents of matter, epitomised by the quest for the Higgs boson[20] and the Theory of Everything, including gravitation.

We now know, however, that there is more to the world than this. First, the "particles" of modern quantum theory are very different from those of classical theory, in that where they are and how they are moving are fundamentally hidden from us. This is the content of the Kochen-Specker theory described above.[p. 26] Thus if we were to think of the universe as being built from the bottom up, starting with the smallest particles and then delineating the large structures that arise from them, we would have to recognise that the resulting edifice would be standing on a shifting ground of unknowable uncertainty.

Furthermore, while quantum theory is well tested and understood at the laboratory level, we shall soon see that at the cosmological level its meaning remains very uncertain. Linked to this is the question of consciousness, which I shall argue is of an essentially different nature from the properties of the physical world. All this undermines the possibility of any "reality" than combines being (actual existents) and form (laws and principles). What it presents us with is not such a reality, but a way of understanding the world far more deeply than before, by harnessing both our fundamental ways of knowing. While "reality" remains an impossible chimera, *being,* coming into existence, is a vital aspect of the universe that is grasped by the relational subsystem of our mind through consciousness; while form is separately analysed through our logical "propositional" subsystem.

2.4 But what about "The Field"?

Since the quantum state is modified by each past event (or "measurement"), and as it also spontaneously evolves in time, as discussed in the next subsection, it carries a sort of history of its past—albeit one that is constantly being overwritten and confused. In this respect the quantum state of the universe is the nearest that real physics gets to a concept invented by some imaginative writers (McTaggart, 2003; Laszlo, 2004; see Clarke & King, 2006) of "The Field" or "The Akashic Field", which is supposed to carry a perfect record of the past. This should not be confused with *quantum fields* in physics, which are structures extended through space and time that are closely related to the Hamiltonian (see the subsection above).

McTaggart also proposes that "The Field" possesses remarkable properties of supporting consciousness as well as preserving memories of past events, etc., and they suggest that this is what quantum theory is about. A similar idea is expressed by Deepak Chopra, who writes, "You are an inseparable part of the field of pure consciousness that gives rise to everything in the physical universe" (Chopra, 2010). This has nothing to do with "field" in its usual sense in physics, though it will turn out (§6.4[p. 139]) that the quantum state of the universe could have aspects of Chopra's hyperbolic expression.

Two questions arise. First, what really is a "field" or a "quantum field" in physics? Secondly, why is it that that two perfectly intelligent writers, and Chopra being a physicist, start writing apparent nonsense? I will address the first of these below, and the second in §7.2.[p. 148]

In 1845 the idea of a "field" emerged from that of a "field of view" (such as the breadth of the area that could be observed through a microscope), when the scientist Michael Faraday referred to the region between the poles of a magnet, in which the magnetic force could be strongly felt, as the "field" of the magnet, later shortened to "the magnetic field". As research continued the "electric field" was similarly described, and the corresponding forces operating in the fields were imagined as invisible "lines of force" pulling on suitable objects within their range. Finally, with the advent of radio waves, it was realised that these two "fields" were inextricably mixed, and so were aspects of a single "electromagnetic field" which could even detach itself from the magnets and batteries which had produced it, and travel through space — or, in one version, propagate as vibrations in an "aether".

The introduction of quantum theory required that all the basic forces could be represented within quantum theory. So, just as an atom when represented in quantum theory had a quantum state which evolved under the influence of a Hamiltonian, so an electromagnetic field had its own state and Hamiltonian. The structure that developed from this idea, in the course of a remarkable collaboration of physicists and mathematicians over many decades, still forms the basis of quantum theory today.

The building blocks for the Hamiltonian are so-called "operators" — a general category that includes the Hamiltonian itself and observables as special cases. All operators "act on" the quantum state, but in a purely abstract, mathematical sense that is distinct from the physical role of, for instance, the Hamiltonian. (An operator changes the state into a different state, but this different state has only an indirect connection with the original state.[21]) Whereas the operators that were used in atomic theory were distinct and localised, the operators for the electromagnetic field formed a continuously varying structure throughout space. This was the "quantum electromagnetic field". As further small-scale physical structures were discovered, they too had their "quantum fields".

It is important to stress that the quantum *state* is something that expresses (albeit in rather a strange way) how things are at a given moment. The Hamiltonian, on the other hand, and the operators that make it up are abstract entities with the same sort of status as the "laws of motion" in classical Newtonian theory. Laws govern the motion of billiard balls, and while you can put billiard balls in a box, it would be a serious category-error to try to put a law of physics in a box. Nonetheless, a law of physics is a very real and powerful thing. Similarly the Hamiltonian for electromagnetism, and the corresponding quantum electromagnetic field, are powerful things, but the substance that they govern is the electromagnetic state.

I suppose the idea of a "law" has a certain numinosity about it, but we don't think of laws as a miasma that eerily wreaths the cosmos like a comic book ghost, and so I see little reason for thinking of quantum fields in this way either.

2.5 Measurement and consciousness

Quantum theory was framed with a laboratory context in mind, and laboratories carry out measurements. What happens, therefore, when the physicist turns to measuring a quantity that has quantum uncertainty? An answer is obtained (otherwise it could not be called a measurement). Moreover, in most cases if the measurement is repeated immediately afterwards the same answer will be obtained: the measurement is reliable. This means that the first measurement removes the uncertainty, which in turn means that the quantum state of the system being investigated has changed, at least as far as the physicist is concerned.

The different interpretations of quantum theory take different positions regarding what happens here. One of the most popular in the early stages of the subject was the idea that a measurement produces an instantaneous change in the quantum state, called "the collapse of the wave-function"[22] — either because of the physical nature of the measurement or, as I discuss in the next section, because a conscious observer is involved. In recent times a reasoned support for this has been put forward by Penrose (2004) involving the way that gravitation alters the space-time structure in the region involved.

Another interpretation which still finds favour is the "many worlds" system of Everett (1957) which proposed that when a measurement occurs the universe, with the observer inside it, splits into a multitude of branches, one for each outcome of the experiment. There are many problems associated with this, if it is taken at face value:

1. It carries the principle of "taking a sledge hammer to crack a nut" to its ultimate extreme.
2. One can always write a formula that expresses the wave function of the universe at a given moment as the sum of an infinite number of components, and to use for the purpose any one of the innumerable processes going on in the universe which might be regarded as a "measurement". But why should the possibility of writing a formula elicit a hyper-cosmological creation event, and which of the many measurements taking place at the time has precedence (or are they all piled on top of each other)?
3. It ignores the problem of how, in strictly physical terms, one can specify what exactly constitutes a "measurement" and how, objectively, the physics singles out the different possible outcomes. In physics one cannot simply say that an event is a measurement because a physicist says it is. It is this, rather than the idea of splitting, which has occupied theoretical work since Everett, with considerable progress having been made.

On the other hand, if we were to interpret the "splitting" not so much as a splitting of the universe, but as a splitting of the minds of those taking part in observation, then we get a more reasonable picture.[23] In this case acts of observation shift a mutually conscious community into a certain strand of awareness within a greater universe — say the symmetrical state from which it appears that the universe came. The total picture is of a sheaf of branching perceptions within a given greater framework.

A key aspect of the nature of a measurement is the apparent distinction between the quantum theory of the system being investigated in the laboratory and the essentially classical theory of the larger universe, including the apparatus part of the laboratory, on which quantum theory would seem to have only an indirect influence. In the laboratory, because of the quantum uncertainty of the system, only statistical laws can be achieved. In the large-scale world, on the other hand, it seems at first glance that universal laws still hold sway.

In the context of this book, a crucial interpretation was presented in 1939 when the German physicist Fritz London, having been forced by the Nazis out of Silesia into France in 1933, joined with Edmond Bauer at the Collège de France to write a pamphlet on quantum measurement. For the first time consciousness was invoked as an element in the interpretation. Following on from the work of Schrödinger in 1926–27 they used the terminology "wave function" to describe the abstract mathematical entity that stood in the place of a possible "quantum world". Paul Langevin, in the preface to their paper, wrote: "The wave function used to describe the object no longer depends solely on the object, as was the case in the classical representation, but, above all, states what the observer knows... For a given object, this function, consequently, is modified in accordance with the information possessed by the observer" (London & Bauer, [1983], p. 218).

The authors then go further to expound this interaction between the wave function and the observer in the course of an observation. This takes place in two steps. First, the microscopic "object" (system) is coupled mechanically with an apparatus having a "pointer" that indicates some property of the system, in a way described entirely by quantum theory. This results in the apparatus entering a state which, when considered on its own, ignoring the system and the larger environments of the apparatus, is of a form known as a "mixture" or "mixed state": a collection of statistics about the probabilities of all the possible outcomes.

> But a coupling, even with a measuring device, is not yet a measurement. A measurement is achieved only when the position of the pointer has been *observed*. It is precisely this increase of knowledge, acquired by observation, that gives the observer the right to choose among the different components of the mixture predicted by the theory, to reject those which are not observed, and to attribute thenceforth to the object a new wave function, that of the pure case which he has found. We note the essential role played by the consciousness of the observer in this transition from the mixture to the pure case.[24] (London & Bauer, [1983], p. 251)

They then go further to specify the nature of this consciousness: "[the observer] has *with himself* relations of a very special character. He possesses a characteristic and quite familiar faculty which we can call the 'faculty of introspection.' He can keep track from moment to moment of his own state"[25] (*ibid.*, p. 252). In other words, according to London and Bauer it is the reflexivity, the self-observation of consciousness, which singles it out for this special role in passing from the quantum realm to the classical realm. In view of the definitions examined in the previous chapter, this could be taken to imply that it is organisms with the sort of consciousness found specifically in human beings (and possibly the highest primates) that bring about the classical world. Later we will see that focussing on subjective consciousness and the relational subsystem gives a much wider scope for consciousness and for the resolution of quantum processes.

This was a dramatic proposal—though it had been foreshadowed by von Neumann's (1932) reference to the "abstract ego" (von Neumann, 1955, p. 421). Not surprisingly, it did not pass uncriticised by subsequent writers. In particular, the influential physicist John Wheeler took a more balanced position (Wheeler, 1981). He accepts that, "Useful as it is under everyday circumstances to say that the universe exists 'out there' independent of us, that view can no longer be upheld. There is a strange sense in which this is a 'participatory universe'." But he continues with a caution regarding "consciousness" in London and Bauer's sense of self-consciousness; for, if this were accepted, it would mean that the creation of the macroscopic world was achieved only by human beings! He insists that "'Consciousness' has nothing whatsoever to do with the quantum process. We are dealing with an event that makes itself known to us by an irreversible act of amplification, by an indelible record, an act of registration." It will turn out that this is an important aspect of the emergence of what we encounter as actual existence.

The idea of London and Bauer is that observation by a human being is an essentially different operation from the amplification and registration of data that Wheeler is referring to. There are many ways of carrying out amplification, but conscious observation is in a class of its own. If London and Bauer are right, we should not expect conscious observation to follow the same laws as the initial stages of measurement, because the former is essentially different—indeed ontologically different—from process.

2.6 Entanglement (spooky action at a distance)[26]

The two phenomena that most distinguish quantum physics from classical physics are uncertainty, discussed in the previous sections, and *entanglement* — the subject of this section. Both are bound up with the nature of those strange objects, "quantum states". I introduced this in section 2.2 as the defining form of any system, regarded as the subject of a laboratory investigation. The quantum state was, and is, sometimes represented as analogous to a wave (see p. 30), albeit in a high-dimensional abstract space; but for many applications, and in particular when discussing entanglement, this is a very misleading analogy. In such cases we have to accept that a quantum state is purely mathematical. Each system is associated with a collection (politely called a *space*) of hypothetical quantum states that it might be in.

Thinking of it this way, quantum states can be handled rather like numbers: with some restrictions they can be multiplied together (but not divided), added together, and multiplied by ordinary numbers and by "complex numbers". The "observables", mentioned in section 2.2, are other mathematical objects that can combine with quantum states to specify information about what happens when you apply a measurement to a system.

Entanglement then works as follows. Suppose we are examining a system like a hydrogen atom, which contains two particles, a proton and an electron. Each one of these is a system in its own right, with an associated space of possible states. In order to set about finding the physics of a hydrogen atom one forms a larger space of states formed by multiplying a state of the electron and a state of the proton. Call all the states formed by this process "basic hydrogen states". To risk a smattering of mathematical symbolism: just as ordinary multiplication is denoted by the sign $\times$ (as in $2 \times 3 = 6$), multiplying states is represented by the sign $\otimes$, so that if e denotes a particular electron state and P denotes a particular proton state, then the expression $e \otimes P$ represents a particular basic hydrogen state, in which both the electron and the proton each also have definite states (e and P) in their own right.

The space of *all* possible hydrogen states is then obtained by a process of multiplying basic hydrogen states by numbers and adding these together.

Suppose now that f and Q are other hydrogen and proton states, respectively. Then the hydrogen atom state[27]

$$e \otimes P + f \otimes Q$$

is an example of an *entangled state* of a hydrogen atom. (NB: it is not a state of 2 hydrogen atoms!) Characteristically, in this case neither the electron nor the proton has a state in their own right. If we conduct an experiment to determine whether the electron is in state e or in state f, either is equally likely to be the result (and similarly for the proton). But if the result found for the electron is e, then an immediately following investigation[28] of the state of the proton will yield P. This is the meaning of "entanglement": the electron and the proton are entangled with each other in a system of mutual correspondence.

In this particular case the electron and the proton are held closely together by electrical attraction and cannot be separated without applying force. But in a case where two such particles can be moved apart without force and without disturbing their states (as is the case with two photons — that is, particles of light) then the same mutual correspondence between their states will apply, however far apart the particles go. This is the phenomenon that Einstein derided as "spooky action at a distance" but which was experimentally verified after his death.

2.7 Quantum theory today

Quantum theory was first developed as a theory of very small objects viewed and manipulated within the context of a laboratory or industrial setting. This is a highly developed and documented discipline taught in every university physics department, and applied in countless practical devices. At this level its bare essentials are little changed since 1927. A key aspect of this sort of quantum theory is that, while the focus of attention is on the small objects, the results are finally registered by comparatively large objects. Large objects are described by the "classical" (i.e. pre-quantum) physics of the 19th century, while the small object is described by the entirely different quantum theory, whose basis I have briefly sketched in the previous section. Usually it is presumed that the large object interacts with the small one in a manner usually depicted as a "measurement", so that the large object becomes an "apparatus". The interaction results in a "pointer" on the apparatus moving so as to indicate the numerical value of some measured property of the small object. (In fact, the large object could equally well be altered in some way that has little, explicitly, to do with measurement, such as forming a picture on a photographic emulsion, where the "pointer movement" is replaced by a "dot formation".) Quantum mechanics then provides a procedure for calculating the probabilities with which the pointer might move to its different possible position.

What makes this a respectable physical theory, as opposed to a rather arbitrary collection of recipes, is quantum measurement theory, expounded by von Neumann (1932) and completed by the ideas of Zeh (1970) and his followers. This supplies a second step in which quantum theory is applied to the apparatus in order to *derive* the way in which it responds to the small object. Thus the whole procedure is brought consistently (though with very significant reservations) under the umbrella of quantum theory.[29, 30]

The work of von Neumann and Zeh shows that internal fluctuations in the apparatus of any experiment measuring quantum effects, and, more importantly, the influence of the external environment on such pieces of apparatus, ensures that the results of an experiment as seen by an observer external to the apparatus obey ordinary classical statistics: quantum theory itself shows that the results displayed by the apparatus are described by *classical* statistics and not by quantum statistics. The process that brings this about, called *decoherence,* accounts for the "Appearance of a classical world" as mapped in detail by Joos *et al.* (2003).

A vital aspect of this phenomenon is the role of entanglement. Whenever two systems interact, they become entangled — essentially permanently so, unless a system is put into a state of its own (or almost so) through special circumstances. The whole of the universe has been swirling around since its emergence and this has provided an opportunity for every element in it to entangle with vast numbers of others. So the world we live in might be thought of as bound together by innumerable threads of entanglement.

But recall from the previous section[p. 42] that a system that is entangled with another one (or more) *does not have a quantum state* in its own right — so that, strictly speaking, the only system with a proper quantum state is the entire universe! (This is one source of motivation for studying quantum cosmology.) But, realistically, a particle that is set up in a particular state for experimental purposes does have a state of its own, at least for a while afterwards — by subatomic standards of time. Fortunately, there is a more general concept of "state" that is always applicable: it is a mathematical construct that, for any measurement on that system and all possible outcomes for that measurement, specifies the probability for obtaining that outcome. I shall refer to this as the *local state*[e. 16] associated with the particular region involved. It turns out that, in general, this is the same thing as a "mixture" or "mixed state", referred to above.[p. 39, e. 18] Sometimes one refers to the state as previously defined as a "pure state". The ubiquity of entanglement means that, strictly speaking, all individual systems only have mixed states, the pure state being an ideal limiting case, or the result of a specific action of consciousness.

A mixed state describing a system combines the "certain uncertainty"[p. 27] of the Heisenberg relations and the

Kochen-Specker theorem with the "uncertain uncertainty" that is always present because of our limited information. What Zeh and his collaborator showed (Joos et al., 2003) is essentially that, when the uncertainty arises from entanglement with the external world, and the system is sufficiently large for this to be dominant, then the mixed state consists almost entirely of uncertain uncertainty. It approximates to a basic object in standard statistics called "the variance-covariance matrix". The classical world has emerged, according to the usual ways of looking at this.

There is an important distinction here between the formation of a mixed state through entanglement and the formation of a new (pure) state as a result of a completed measurement (on the "collapse" interpretation). The first (the mixed state) can be thought of as the appearance that the unchanged state presents for measurements that are restricted to the system under investigation, with the global quantum state of the universe remaining pure. The second (the pure collapsed state) is a new state that is valid for all subsequent measurements.

The success of the work of Zeh and others has tended to eclipse the more fundamental problem that has remained untouched, namely how it is that one particular result emerges from one particular experiment. When a physicist performs an experiment, a result is obtained. As the experiment is repeated, so the various results start to exhibit a pattern that can be described by statistics, which are explained by quantum theory; but where do the individual events come from? It will emerge that something like London and Bauer's use of consciousness can explain this, but only if we succeed in understanding what is meant by "consciousness" and how it works. This will be our goal in the rest of this book.

2.8 Quantum cosmology

In the previous section[p. 44, e. 29] I described how decoherence—the formation from a quantum state of a local statistical mixed state—arose from considering the unknowable factors influencing the phases of quantum states in the process of a physics experiment, and how the influence of the environment on the experimental apparatus played a role in this. The question arises, how widely does one need to take "the environment"? Since the quantum effect of entanglement (section 2.5) arises whenever two particles or systems interact with each other in any way, and in general continues however far apart they may subsequently move, there is a case for going the whole hog and taking the entire universe as the context for understanding quantum theory. This is quantum cosmology—for which a digression is now required. I will first give a synopsis of the history of cosmology, followed by a discussion of its implications for quantum theory.

Cosmology is the study of the large-scale structure of the entire universe. Information about this comes from astronomical instruments: at first optical telescopes built on remote mountain peaks so as to minimise the distortions of the atmosphere and the lights of cities; then from 1937 the familiar "upturned dish" of the radio telescope sensing objects too far away for their visible light to be detected; and now instruments mounted in satellites and so completely free from atmospheric interference. Observations from these instruments convey not only pictures of distant objects, but, from a detailed analysis of the light received, the sort of physical processes going on in them and, by observing the "blue shift" or "red shift" of radiation from its initial colour to a bluer or redder colour, the speed with which they may be moving towards us or away from us.

The key point in these observations is that, since light takes time to travel from its source to us, the more distant the object is the earlier is the time at which we are seeing it. So observations of very distant objects are a way of seeing into the remote past. Thus astronomical observations tell us what objects there are, how they are distributed in space, and how they have changed since earlier times.

The single most important observation in cosmology is the discovery by Edwin Hubble in 1929 that the more distant galaxies are moving away from us with a speed that increases with their distance, suggesting that the universe as a whole is expanding. An apparently obvious consequence of this is that the universe is steadily becoming less dense with its galaxies steadily more scattered. Extrapolating backwards in time, it would seem that the universe started in a very dense state at a calculable time in the past.

A diversion from this conclusion occurred in 1948 when Fred Hoyle pointed out that this need not be the case if matter was continuously created so as to "fill in the gaps" left by this global expansion. He called this the "steady state theory" and jokingly referred to the mainstream opinion as the "big bang theory" — a joke that has firmly stuck, despite its inappropriateness for a theory in which the universe appeared in complete silence. It would be better to call the initiation of the universe "the Big Question Mark" because we know nothing about it and have neither language nor theory to speak about it.[31] Subsequent observation, however, eventually eliminated Hoyle's theory. So the universe is evolving.

The second most important observation in cosmology (Smoot, 2007) started by accident in 1964. Two Bell Labs engineers, Arno Penzias and Robert Wilson (1965), were trying to improve their reception of high-frequency radio signals (microwaves) bounced off "echo" satellites. Their reception was hampered by an unvarying signal coming uniformly from all directions, for which they could find no explanation. At the same time Robert Dicke and collaborators at Princeton University were predicting that such radiation could arise from heat radiation emitted very early in the universe and red shifted to microwaves by the time it reached us. Specifically, the radiation was coming from the period when the universe was about 377,000 years old (it is now roughly 13,700,000,000 years old) and its matter content, as a result of continuous cooling, had changed from a mixture of free protons and electrons — which was opaque to electromagnetic radiation — to a universe full of hydrogen gas formed from the combination of these particles, which is transparent. This clearing of the "fog" then allowed the natural heat radiation being emitted by the matter to stream through the universe with little subsequent interaction with matter. This moment (or rather, this comparatively short period) of the clearing is called the "recombination[32] epoch", when protons and electrons combined.

A series of satellite observations of this radiation were made, the latest being the results from the WMAP satellite that was launched in 2001 and has been sending back data ever since. The radiation is uniform except for fluctuations of one part in 100,000, indicating that at the time when it was emitted the universe was this uniform. This confirms theoretical predictions that in the course of evolution of the cosmos after the state examined by WMAP, small fluctuations in the density and temperature of the universe grew because of the influence of gravity into progressively larger fluctuations and eventually into the stars that we see around us.[33]

WMAP also provided indirect information about the state of the universe before it became transparent, in the form of very small large-scale trends in this radiation. These matched the predictions of current theory, implying that at much earlier times there were slight oscillations of the universe whose effects modified the radiation when it was released in the recombination epoch. This information from the detailed nature of the fluctuations in the microwave background radiation (N. Jarosik *et al.*, 2011) is consistent with current theory: that as one traces back through the history of the universe, it is seen to be more and more perfectly symmetrical, all its departures from a symmetrical state appearing in the course of its evolution. It seems that the universe emerged from the Big Question Mark in a state of complete symmetry.

This brings us to quantum physics. On conventional theory, the oscillations and fluctuations that we see in the WMAP data, which eventually grew to produce the whole structure of the universe with its galaxies, stars, and planets, arose as quantum fluctuations in the symmetrical quantum state of the entire universe. As Brian Greene (2006) put it, *"galaxies are nothing but quantum mechanics writ large across the sky."* This idea underpins the steadily growing discipline of quantum cosmology which studies in detail the evolution of the cosmos when it was a quantum entity with a spatially symmetrical quantum state.

There is just one snag with this. If one starts with a completely symmetrical quantum state and allows it to evolve under the equally symmetrical laws of quantum physics (as specified by the Hamiltonian—see §2.3), then the state stays completely symmetrical. No fluctuations. No galaxies?

One possible way out is that, when we succeed in pushing back our theories into an understanding of the Big Question Mark, in which time and space themselves emerge, then we will discover something richer than pure symmetry. But, despite many ongoing attempts (string theory, M-theory, and so on) there are no theories that remotely match the universe as we see it. The other path to follow is to examine this notion of "quantum fluctuations".

In fact, quantum fluctuations from a symmetrical state are very easy to observe. If one enters a light-proof room that is uniformly lit by a very dim and very uniform light and takes a photograph with a fast film (or views the scene with an image intensifier) then the resulting picture is full of random speckles, called photon noise, produced by individual photons arriving at the film or the detector. What is happening is that a particular sort of measurement is being made by the photographic plate on the light that is filling the room. This involves the individual molecules of the silver compound used in the plate, the plate being set up to measure the intensity of the light from different directions. It is a quantum measurement subject to quantum uncertainty, and hence the result fluctuates randomly. The act of making a measurement breaks the symmetry of the quantum state of the light in a random way.

Now let us return to quantum cosmology, and the proposal—now supported by good evidence (Jarosik *et al.*, 2011)—that what we are observing are quantum fluctuations. These arise as a result of observations. So who is measuring the universe so that it produces fluctuations in the first microseconds of its history, and when are they doing it?

This quantum state of the universe includes everything; it has no observer standing outside the universe to measure it. Some might argue that God, or "universal consciousness", was such an observer, but this would (literally) be a "*deus ex machina*": a character in a drama arbitrarily brought in, with no coherent justification, in order to tie up the loose ends of a tricky situation. In fact I will be arguing for something like this much later in this book, but only after developing the necessary physics to justify it. Quantum theory as it is normally practised, however, has no such resource. The state of the universe in quantum cosmology is destined to evolve smoothly in time with no "collapse of the wave function" or observation to jolt it into a different path. A new interpretation of quantum theory is required in order to justify the very promising ideas that are emerging from quantum cosmology.

The first, and most influential, step in providing such an interpretation was taken by Wheeler (Wheeler & Klauder, 1972). To the question "who is observing the early universe?" he gave the simple answer: "we are — now"! Let us unpack this rather disturbing proposition. Wheeler favours the "collapse" interpretation of quantum theory, though he rejects the idea that it is specifically consciousness that is involved), so that making an observation, whether of the universe or of a tiny particle, determines certain properties of the thing observed and effectively alters its state so that further measurements will be consistent with the one just made, as described in §2.5.p. 36

When it comes to the time at which the collapse takes place, we might suspect that it takes place at the same time as the observation. But relativity theory shows that the concept "at the same time as" cannot in itself be defined because "time" is something that depends on which observer is measuring it (a fact that is well-known to designers of satellite navigation devices, which have to allow for this problem). The only observer-independent time-relationships are past, future, space-like, and null (on the borderline between past or future and space-like). This means that the ambiguity manifest in quantum theory through the different optional variations extends, in the collapse interpretation, to an ambiguity in the time of collapse. (This will be reflected in the histories interpretation reviewed below.) We are free to assign any chronology to the region of space-time where the collapse occurs (except the future because we would then be able actually to observe a delay between our observation and the collapse). There is thus no inconsistency in assuming that, as result of our (or others') observation of the early universe at the time of recombination, quantum fluctuations take place *at that time and place where they are observed.* These fluctuations then give rise to galaxies and hence to ourselves; we create ourselves by making the observation that gives rise to ourselves! Wheeler would illustrate this by drawing a "U", for "universe", looking at itself, like the sketch below.

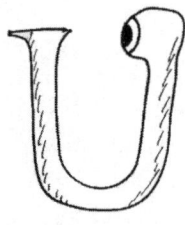

This presentation stresses the most paradoxical version of the proposal; but on closer examination it starts to look more reasonable, though more complex. If we were to take the view, as in fact Wheeler did, that it is not consciousness that performs an observation, but rather it is anything that forms a permanent *record* of some aspect of the current state of affairs, then observation becomes a continuous process that begins from the moment of recombination. When the slight fluctuations that were present implicitly in the state of the universe reached the modest size needed for them to be reasonably stable, this itself became a record, one which then was augmented and expanded in the subsequent history of the cosmos, of which we ourselves constitute a tiny part.

We will see in the next section that this account is very close to the histories interpretation of quantum theory treated below. It suffers, however, from the same problems. It demonstrates that the symmetrical state of the universe at the Big Question Mark contained, as a component within it, a history with fluctuations such as we observe, and that this potential could be "liberated" by the subsequent formation of a record. But it also contains a mind-bogglingly vast array of histories, most of them probably totally chaotic or so different from "our" universe as to be totally inconceivable. Maybe the version we see is indeed only one of many, but unless we find some criterion for whittling down the possibilities, we cannot actually explain anything about our version of the world. We can only say "we're here because we're here." To put it another way, using the context of the notion of observation developed earlier, how is it that a statistical ensemble of outcomes (generated by decoherence) turns into one particular outcome? How does one pass from the *possibility* expressed by statistics to the *actual being* of an event?

2.9 Histories: collapse without collapse

In this section I will set out the "consistent histories interpretation" of quantum theory, which, as just noted, is a natural development of Wheeler's picture. This influential new interpretation was published by Griffiths in (1984) and analysed in more detail by Dowker and Kent (1996). Their basic formalism has been further discussed and developed since then, and my account here is as much, or more, my own reinterpretation than Griffiths' original intention. I will refer to these variations in general as simply "the histories interpretation".

The basic idea is that the universe smoothly and deterministically evolves as specified by its Hamiltonian (see §2.3). What we actually observe, however, are *histories* of observations. In a sense "histories" constitute an extra layer of physics in addition to the "quantum state". The two concepts are distinct, though of course closely linked. A history consists of a sequence of *propositions*: mathematical representations, observations, or measurements with the particular property that they can only produce one of two outcomes, usually interpreted as "yes" or "no". Propositions are yes/no questions about the universe. This stipulation is a mathematical ruse rather than a real restriction: any more complex situation can (from a strictly propositional standpoint, in the psychological sense!) be built up from a combination of propositions. This use of propositions will play a large role when we consider logic, later on.[p. 92]

In standard logic, every proposition P is associated with the corresponding negation $\sim P$, one being true precisely when the other is false; and in practical terms the process of deciding whether P is true or false is identical to the process of deciding whether $\sim P$ is false or true. We can think of a history (a sequence of propositions) either as a *history template,* specifying a sequence of questions each of which has two possible outcomes, or as a *history outcome* specifying that what actually happened was the verification of a particular list of propositions. A history outcome can be thought of as a rather jerky movie of the universe from the point of view of a single observer, and a history template as a similar movie but with two alternative scenes available for each frame, with the facility for feeding in at each step what the actual outcomes of the propositions are.

The rules of quantum theory, including the action of the Hamiltonian, assign to each history template a probability of producing any given history outcome (a sequence of "yes"s and "no"s). A set of histories is called "consistent" if these probabilities obey the proper laws of statistics — something that happens if the propositions are sufficiently far apart in time to enable decoherence (section 2.6) of the measuring apparatus(es) to happen in between observations.[34]

The basic advantage of this approach is the fact that it is not necessary to assume that the entire universe collapses each time an observation is made; all that is required is the process by which the probability of each observation is conditioned by all its previous observations. It is thus a very "clean" interpretation with minimal ontological assumptions. It has the drawback, however, that it does not provide a concrete picture of what is going on: what exactly is the physical connection between the "observer" and the smoothly evolving universe? What would be the meaning of a history template that was *not* "consistent"?

A particularly interesting variant of this approach was given by Hartle (1991), called by him "generalised quantum theory", in which full allowance was made for the effect of the geometry of general relativity on this picture, in a way that enlarges the idea of observations being made at "different times" or "the same time". In Newtonian theory there is an absolute concept of time, so that given any two happenings A and B — such as, for instance, physics experiments or conscious human acts of perceptions — either A is before B, or B is before A, or A and B overlap in time (and in this Newtonian case there are definite times at which one or the other starts or stops). As we noted in the last section,[p. 51] however, in relativity theory there is a fourth possibility of A and B being "space-like connected": there is no time relation (past/future) between them. In his version of the histories interpretation, instead of dealing with a linear sequence of propositions at successive times, Hartle uses a scattering of propositions over space-time, each having a "thickness in time" so that each proposition occupies an extended space-time region. A space-like connection between regions is allowed in addition to "before" and "after", but overlapping in time is not allowed (see [e. 35] for a diagram and details).

This approach deals with the erroneous idea, often found even in scientific writing, that when an observation is made on one of a pair of entangled particles (§2.5), the other "immediately" changes its state; a postulate which, as we have noted[p. 51] has no meaning in a cosmological situation where, strictly speaking, no global time is defined. In Hartle's version nothing is said about what happens to the individual systems being examined: it is only when the results of all aspects of the experiment are brought together that one can see how the two entangled particles have changed in relation to each other.

One way of imagining Hartle's histories — I shall call them "generalised histories" to distinguish them from Griffiths' version — pictures them as hovering over a cosmic space-time that supplies only the basic ground of being, unaffected by the vagaries of consciousness. Conscious happenings are part of the business of histories. Histories are shaped by considerations of logical connection between the happenings (not necessarily using classical logic) and by the constraints of the space-time ground, which supply probabilities. Hartle generalises the histories interpretation so as to provide a probability for any generalised history, but this still leaves open the question of how one passes from a probability to an actuality: what actually happens may be the result of the interplay of physical constraints and active consciousness. We will return to this question later.

This picture of moments of awareness scattered over space and time, all interconnecting with each other, all contributing to a global probability distribution and thence—as we will discuss later—to consciousness, is strongly reminiscent of the "Web of Indra", a fabled net with jewels at every knot, in which each jewel reflects the images of all the others. (In its full detail, this story appears to be modern.[36])

Hartle's interpretation (in the form in which I am presenting it here) has the unexpected role of introducing a second source of decoherence, in addition to that described above.[p. 44] Its basis is the fact that an experiment, or a perception by consciousness, cannot happen instantaneously: the parts of the seat of consciousness involved have to act coherently, and they cannot operate more rapidly than the time taken for light to travel from one part to another. This is another outcome of there being no such thing as "simultaneity" in the cosmos. In both special and general relativity there is no fixed clock that can define whether or not two things happen simultaneously. The only exception is the case of the symmetrical quantum cosmos that is the underlying state of quantum cosmology, when the symmetry and smoothness of the universe allows one to define a global time. This means that any observation or perception is effectively averaged over the duration of an extended region, an averaging whose effect is equivalent to the production of decoherence and the formation of a mixed state with purely classical components (Clarke, 2001). It is this local mixed state that contributes to the overall probability of a generalised history, while on this interpretation the quantum state of the entire universe remains unchanged by the measurement.

Hartle's approach is the interpretation that best makes sense of the interplay between the cosmos and small-scale observations, although it is rather clumsy in application. It is an interpretation that takes into account general relativity and quantum cosmology; it automatically handles the finite duration in time that is taken by an observation or the formation of a conscious perception; and it avoids introducing *ad hoc* processes such as the collapse of the state or the splitting of the universe (or of strands of awareness).

It has, however, one critical flaw, in that it depicts a history as a collection of observing-situations, for which probabilities for different sets of outcomes will be calculated, situated within a *given* space-time (the cosmos). But the structure of space-time cannot be "given" in advance of what happens within it, because according to *general* relativity events in space-time react back on the geometry of space-time and modify it.[37] In order to implement this generalised quantum theory, therefore, one would have to use an integrated theory that not only derived histories from quantum theory and space-time; but, conversely, derived the evolution of space-time from the outcomes of histories.

Viewed in practical terms the implementation of such a programme seems even more problematic, because the back-reaction from quantum events onto space-time will involve understanding how quantum theory handles the dynamics of space-time. This is a completely unsolved problem, which is generally regarded as requiring a totally new approach.

We should note that this argument—suggesting that a conventional approach to quantum theory breaks down at the point when quantum events interact with the space-time structure of general relativity—reaches, by a different route, the conclusion supported by Penrose (1989, 2004),[p. 121] which leads him to argue that consciousness itself plays a decisive role in the detailed dynamics of general relativity. Here we can only make tentative steps towards the major challenge of solving the most intractable issues of physics and philosophy in interaction with each other. Scientific work over the last 100 years has been a preliminary limbering up for this ultimate task ahead!

2.10 Selection in quantum cosmology

> 'Once upon a time there were three little sisters,' the Dormouse began in a great hurry; 'and their names were Elsie, Lacie, and Tillie; and they lived at the bottom of a well...
> And so these three little sisters—they were learning to draw, you know—'
> 'What did they draw?' said Alice, quite forgetting her promise.
> 'Treacle,' said the Dormouse...
> Alice did not wish to offend the Dormouse again, so she began very cautiously: 'But I don't understand. Where did they draw the treacle from?'
> 'You can draw water out of a water-well,' said the Hatter; 'so I should think you could draw treacle out of a treacle-well—eh, stupid?'
> 'But they were in the well,' Alice said to the Dormouse, not choosing to notice this last remark.
> 'Of course they were', said the Dormouse; ' —well in.'

This quotation from *Alice's adventures in Wonderland* is mirrored by the problem of quantum cosmology: substitute "experimental quantum cosmologists" for Elsie *et al.* and "cosmos" for "well", and one can see that theorising the cosmos when you are in it has much the same problems as drawing treacle from a treacle well when you are in it. And we are indeed "well in" the cosmos.

In the case of a theoretical physicist, call him the Hatter, who is outside the system he is examining, the success of his theory depends on his finding that his own readings of what is going on in the system do indeed match his predictions for the system being investigated and the nature of his apparatus. Similarly, in the case of a quantum cosmologist, call her Elsie, the success of her current theory of cosmology depends on her finding that her readings of what is going on in the cosmos do indeed match her predictions for the cosmos as observed by current astronomy. There is, however, a crucial difference: while the Hatter can imagine the system to be set in any way that is within his ingenuity, and then choose different processes for observing it, Elsie is stuck with the cosmos we've got, which includes herself and her observation as an integral part of the system itself. The whole concept of "observation" is skewed from the start.

The solution to this is to use a principle that generalises the idea of observation so as to include observation both from outside (the laboratory experiment) and from within (cosmology). In the case of observation of a system by an external observer, and speaking of it very formally, the concept of observation defines two things: first, it defines a particular *collection of properties* of the system (such as a set of possible positions for a particle or an object) which are mutually exclusive (so that precisely one result will emerge from an examination of the system); and second, in conjunction with the quantum state of the system, it assigns probabilities to these properties that quantify how likely each one is to be realised. Thus the concept of an observation *selects* a collection of one or more aspects of the system, and then quantifies the likelihoods of their possible values.

One way of going beyond external observation is then to apply the idea of selection to the wider realm of quantum cosmology, based on the condition that the universe is subject to observation *from within*. If possible this development ought to be quantified, so that in principle it should be possible to derive a probability for various outcomes to occur. It would seem that this could provide a test of our cosmological theories, and a way in to understanding how a homogeneous universe might give rise to observers, and hence to the growth of fluctuations necessary to give rise to observers.

The first attempt at formulating this idea was made by Donald (1990), who focussed on the brain. Simplifying this to networks of switches, he thus proposed that the essential ingredient of human observation was some sort of switching network that could make logical deductions. Clearly the drawback to this approach is not merely that it neglects the subjective aspect of consciousness that I have developed (an aspect which many authors would, however, regard as irrelevant) but also that, by focussing on the mechanics of "switching", it would seem to make an automatic telephone exchange, for example, the paradigm of an observer.

A more appropriate implementation of this selection approach was later taken by Page (2001), who argued that the minimum requirement for there to be a perceiver of the cosmos—an inhabitant of the dormouse's "well" that can respond to the cosmos in a meaningful way—is that some part of the cosmos, at some moment in time[38] is capable of "sensation". This requirement, he claims, is more fundamental than having mind or consciousness or a continuing history of perception. Recognising that defining "sensation" will require a major investigation in its own right, he does not give a precise definition himself. If this be accepted as a starting point, then we can ask whether there is an interpretation of quantum cosmology under which it is possible to extract from a given cosmological model a probability for there being sensation in that universe.

In principle this makes sense. If we could plausibly give, in precise terms, a physical specification of what a chunk of the cosmos has to be like, in relation to the rest of the cosmos, for it to be "sensing", then quantum theory, by analogy with the way it handles observations, provides us with a formula for calculating the probabilities of the different perceptions that arose.

Distinctively, Page argues not for sensation as an ongoing history, but as a discrete event. The totality of all sensation, in any sensate being at any moment, comprises a memory that is regarded as "past", an impression that is regarded as "present", and expectations of what is called "future". But this is all sensed in the present: we do not sense the past, but rather a present memory that is attributed to the past.

This point is developed in the debates about the nature of time in the philosophical tradition of phenomenology (Merleau-Ponty, 1962 [1945]; Bergson, 1910 [1889]) which explores the meaning of the immediate experience of time, as distinct from its sanitised version delivered by rational analysis. In the terminology of the next chapter, they are bringing in a level of relational knowing that is essential for understanding consciousness, going beyond the rational level of Page.

Subsequently this approach to time was developed by Heidegger, particularly in his late lecture *Zeit und Sein* (Heidegger, 1969 [1962]). Here Heidegger, meditating on time as grasped by consciousness (via a form of knowing through relationship that will be explored in the next chapter), refers to time as "four dimensional": in addition to present, past, and future there is the fourth dimension of "the mutual offering to one another of future, past and present, that is, to their own unity".[39] This affirms and elucidates our instinctive feeling that we are not experiencing an isolated momentary "now", nor even a simple "flow", but participating in a rich process.

Acknowledging time as process in this way justifies our regarding our experiences as part of a history, even though at the rational level of mathematical physics we can only represent a history as a sequence of events. So we can combine Heidegger, Page, and Hartle and regard Hartle's generalised histories, described in the previous section, as a selection approach. The fundamental underlying universe is the symmetrical universe of quantum cosmology; what we can actually know is represented by histories of Hartle's form: sequences of glimpses of the universe, selected by their nature of "sensation".

What gives a histories approach its predictive power is its assignment of a probability to each history outcome. At its simplest this imposes the constraint that we can only observe history outcomes that are possible, in that they have a probability greater than zero, in addition to the constraint that we have drawn from Page of being "sensational". In practice, however, the situation is more complex than this. The number of possible histories within the entire universe that satisfy these conditions is still vast; indeed if the universe is infinite in space and time, there will be uncountably many possible histories, each with uncountably many possible history outcomes. Criteria are then needed to aggregate these possibilities in such a way that "well behaved" probabilities can be assigned to each aggregate, which seems hard with only the condition of sensation. Yet here we are, enjoying one particular instance of this plenitude. A probability of zero is no bar to existence. Is the only outcome of this lengthy discussion the statement that "we're here because we're here"?[40]

This impasse encourages us to bring in considerations of consciousness in order to complete a picture which, without it, explains very little. Introducing "sensation" without referring to consciousness does not seem to achieve much; whereas the introduction of consciousness and the relational way of knowing opens up a whole new methodology of increasing our understanding. It can provide insight into the relationship between the symmetrical cosmological model that is taken as our starting point and the universe with "sensation" in it.

Philosophically, the selection approach of Donald and Page is an attempt to avoid the question of *being*, in the sense in which one says that the universe *is*, that it *exists*. One could also phrase this in terms of "reality". The selection approach hopes that some sort of mechanism whereby the universe can pull itself up by its own boot straps will generate existence out of an idea. At the root of the difficulties of quantum cosmology is the problem that physics has no notion of "being" because this belongs to our relational way of knowing, while physics belongs to the propositional way. There is also, however, a technical issue: the notion of "sensation" is a narrow one applicable only to our propositional conception of life, whereas the existence and nature of the cosmos is vastly more general. As we develop the notion of consciousness we will see that this also, in its essence, is profoundly general and at a level with being.

2.11 Between knowing and being

Hartle's approach[p. 54] above, gives us ideas for tackling the question[p. 53] which I phrased as "how does one pass from the *possibility* of statistics to the *actual being* of an event?" But the devil is in the details, and the physics that we have at present has not been developed in the direction that is needed if we are to make concrete the ideas that I have been floating.

Let us approach this through the notion of "reality", a topic that tends to be either dismissed or approached rather loosely and uncritically within the sciences. In §2.1 we have already noted that from Plato until Kant it had been assumed that a clear line could be drawn between reality and illusion or hearsay. Plato, and those of a Platonic bent, held that naïve observation through our unassisted or untrained senses yielded a shifting, unreliable *appearance* of the world, while intellectual analysis (especially by philosophers!) yielded *reality*. As far as science ("natural philosophy") was concerned, this view continued until the end of the nineteenth century. But as we have discussed, Kant shifted the focus of philosophy to our own capacity to know, thereby adopting the position that the reality of something *in and for itself* was unknowable for the observer. Some workers in quantum theory have taken up a similar position with regard to their subject, most notably Niels Bohr (§2.1) and the respected philosopher of quantum theory Bernard d'Espagnat (2003 [1994]) who concludes that the reality of quantum entities is a "hidden reality".

Despite all this, the alluring assumption of "reality" creeps into our thinking. If quantum theory predicts that the state of a large piece of apparatus is a classical probability distribution, and if we do in fact subsequently see that the apparatus is in a completely well-defined configuration, then surely this means that this situation was "really" there all the time. Why should we doubt this in the case of the laboratory apparatus, when we accept the reality of, for instance, the orientation of a die that is rolled and then concealed? Why indeed. But is quantum theory, perhaps, telling us that in neither case can we assume that a real configuration exists, without some justification for doing so?

Quantum theory forces us to accept that, at least in the case of small systems, it is logically inconsistent to assume the simultaneous reality of all the properties of a system (the Kochen-Specker theorem) and that we therefore need to justify the reality of *any* property of the system. Reality thus becomes dependent on context, and the real existence of some property of the system, its "being", depends on a particular form of "knowing". Quantum cosmology goes further and extends this to the whole world, without having to depend on an ambiguous concept of "small system".

The weighty element here is "knowing". Wheeler is surely right to deride the idea that the whole cosmos is dependent on the particular sort of knowing that is exercised by *Homo sapiens* at one epoch of time on one insignificant planet. This would be absurdly arbitrary! But equally, one cannot rely on the vague notion of "an act of registration" (§2.4, Wheeler, 1981): in the early phase of the universe that we are now directly observing with the WMAP satellite, a phase of dynamic ripples within an otherwise uniform gaseous universe, there were no "records" or distinct clear-cut "systems" (Zeh, 1970) . But it would be almost as arbitrary to demand that the universe should reach the stage where, say, the formation of solid planets occurred somewhere before a real universe could emerge. The early intimation by London and Bauer (1983, section 2.4) that "consciousness" is involved is highly relevant; but for this not to be equally arbitrary it must involve a sense of this word that is applicable much more widely than to creatures like human beings.

This sets key themes for the future development of the foundations of quantum theory in the light of consciousness: we need to bring together and reconcile consciousness with quantum theory on the ground of the histories interpretation and a selection process applied to Hartle's generalised history interpretation, bearing in mind the points established in the previous chapter.

Synopsis

- Classical physics considered that measurements could be extended to a complete knowledge of reality; while quantum physics placed strict limits on this possibility.
- The Kochen-Specker theorem showed that, for all except the simplest systems, it was not logically possible for all measurable quantities to have exact values simultaneously, let alone for them to be measurable. This confirms Kant's insight that "the world" is as

- much a product of our particular ways of knowing as it is of the cosmos.
- A fundamental aspect of a system in quantum theory is its quantum state, which determines the probabilities for measurement outcomes.
- Some interpretations hold that the quantum state "collapses" on measurement. A subset of these attribute collapse to the consciousness of the observer. London and Bauer attribute collapse to consciousness.
- A mixture combines quantum uncertainty with classical lack of knowledge (uncertain uncertainty).
- When two systems are entangled only the combined system (not the individual ones) has a quantum state. Measurements on the individual systems are then correlated; measurements on one of the systems behave as if that system was in a mixture. Entanglement with the environment produces (in this sense) mixtures that replicate classical physics.
- Quantum cosmology regards the whole universe as a highly symmetrical quantum system. The emergence from this of a variegated natural world is hard to explain: front runners involve selection of components of the state of the universe by sensate beings or through histories.
- There is a need for a concept of consciousness that acknowledges the insight of London and Bauer while being sufficiently general to make sense of quantum cosmology.
- For further reading see Kumar (2008).

Three

The Mind and its Logics: Knowing

We are conscious through our mind. While consciousness is the fundamental, irreducible source of knowing, doing, and being, mind is the network of processes through which these faculties operate. The "hardware" for operating these processes is the brain. Putting it simply, mind is thinking. We now know a lot about the mind by analysing it with psychological methods and by learning how brain activities are correlated with different mental processes; but mind is so complex that we have probably barely scratched its surface. Systematic descriptions of the mind are therefore necessarily rather crude, but they are still vital for understanding human beings. One description constantly used in this book treats the mind as if it were made up of two main systems which I call propositional and relational – as well as a number of minor systems.

Logic can be thought of either as a recommendation for how we ought to think if we are to do so more effectively, or as a simplified broad-brush description of how we actually think. The first of these aspects of mind gave rise to "conventional" logic developed from Aristotle onwards, while the second has given rise in recent times to unconventional logics. Some of these will turn out to be relevant to understanding quantum theory.

3.1 The reinvention of knowing

We now turn from physics to philosophy, but with a view to uniting the two later. In order to give more substance to these topics, it is helpful to recall the core idea of Kant's philosophy as I described them in chapter 1: that our understanding of the world is shaped and limited by our own human capacities for knowing and understanding. Kant was primarily concerned with our thinking (intellectual and cognitive) capacities rather than the capacities of our senses. The latter have, of course, been greatly extended since Kant's time by progressively more sophisticated scientific instruments, but the former, the range of our thinking, has in its essence changed little — and may even have contracted. From this Kantian core, I have argued that our knowledge of the world is to be seen not as the unfolding of absolute reality, but as the product of a constantly developing interaction between our human capacities and the greater universe of which we are part.

Over the last 20 years, a new dimension has been opened on this concept of knowledge. A starting point was the approach of Michel Foucault (2003, p. 7) who suggested that we switch attention from abstract knowledge to the process of knowing by which we reach this knowledge, and to the social contexts within which this knowing takes place. The knowledge of those whose knowing takes place from within a context of political power will differ from the knowledge of those outside the circles of power. Moreover, some of these latter "subjugated ways of knowing" may preserve traditional practical experience that has been lost by those in power.

More recently, an even more fundamental insight into the process of human knowing has developed through the work of McGilchrist (2009), mentioned in chapter 1, and the complementary approaches of Teasdale and Barnard (1993), each exploring a basic duality present in all human knowing, of whatever culture and context. Teasdale and Barnard worked within a cognitive psychology unit examining such things as how easily different events were recalled from memory, how memories interfered with each other, how rapidly different sorts of information were processed, and so on. On the basis of this they suggested that the simplest and most effective way of understanding our basic mental processing was to regard it as arising from several distinct but interacting subsystems within the brain, each having its own memory store and each "encoding" information in a different way. Each subsystem took, as it were, a different perspective on the situation. There was no single "I" bringing together the whole thing, but rather two primary meaning-making subsystems which they called the *implicational* and the *propositional*. The two constantly exchanged information with each other, giving the impression of a single system. The implicational subsystem viewed events in the light of how they impinged on the self: whether they were threatening or beneficial. The propositional subsystem analysed the situation more objectively, in a way that was closely related to language. It was logical in the popular sense of that word. We approach the world both through personally significant stories and through logical analysis.

Ian McGilchrist approached the mind quite differently, from a background of neuropsychiatry and cultural history, but came up with a very similar picture. Data from neuropsychiatry indicated that the propositional subsystem was particularly associated with the left hemisphere of the brain and the implicational subsystem with the right hemisphere. One important shift of emphasis was the demonstration that the implicational/right hemisphere-dominated subsystem was particularly concerned with our *relationships* connecting us with people and things in the world. McGilchrist's work shows that similarity between the information flow between the hemispheres and that between the primary subsystems is no coincidence: but neither is it evidence of an identity or an equivalence. It is at least clear, however, that there is a strong correspondence. From now on I will call the right-dominated/implicational subsystem *the relational,* and the left-dominated/language-linked subsystem *the propositional*.

This dual model of the mind clarifies the nature of our self-consciousness—the reflexive consciousness of the "I" as described in §1.4. The basic experiential data for this is acquired by the relational subsystem, which is constantly monitoring events that impinge on personal status, and so on the self-model, "I". Self-consciousness then arises from the inspection of this data by the propositional subsystem. It is this inspection of one subsystem by another that makes self-consciousness such a distinctively human phenomenon.

Subjective consciousness—the basic consciousness that is my main concern in this book—ranges over both subsystems. This is explicit in Teasdale and Barnard's model in which consciousness has a role in initiating information transfers between the two subsystems. In McGilchrist's model consciousness on the relational side is a strong qualitative direct awareness, whereas on the propositional side this is overlaid by the reflexive understanding of self-consciousness. The two different emphases here are not, however, contradictory. Both subsystems contribute equally to "what it is like to be", and both are ultimately controlled by consciousness in this sense. But when it comes to grasping what consciousness (in the subjective sense) really is, the relational subsystem definitely acts the most clearly. Unlike the propositional subsystem, it is not distracted by the desire to pin down what consciousness does. Thus we need to draw on this subsystem particularly in order to understand consciousness.

If we now draw on the Kantian idea that the world as we conceive it is inevitably a reflection of our ways of knowing, then the dual structure of our knowing suggests that we will see the world as having, as it were, two sides or aspects to it: an analytical side which seems logical and mechanical, and a meaningful side which inspires us or appals us.[41] The dominant, scientific way of knowing in our Western culture is, however, committed to the idea that, really, there is only one true aspect of the world, namely the propositional, scientific aspect. The other side, the concern of the relational subsystem, is regarded simply as our own bodily emotional reaction to the "real" scientific situation, a reaction which, it is claimed, can be fully understood through a rational analysis of our physiology and the rest of the world. On this way of thinking, the relational way of understanding our behaviour remains a convenient shortcut for describing how we choose a partner or decide what to cook for dinner,[42] but it can always be rephrased in physical terms.

We need not rehearse just how effective this scientific approach has been. It is progressively solving all the problems that come within its grasp, with two exceptions that never quite seem to be tied up: the nature of consciousness and a comprehensive interpretation of quantum theory—exceptions that keep being linked, despite repeated claims that the problems have been solved. There is a widespread idea that consciousness plays some sort of a role in quantum theory, but details as to how this happens are sadly lacking. The problem is that not only does the idea lack detail when it comes to the consciousness side of the interaction with quantum theory, but also many aspects of our concepts of consciousness are incompatible with the world-views of science—coming as they do from two different mental subsystems. Science seeks rigorous logical accounts of the objective world while consciousness is subjective and, at least as far as its relational side is concerned, it does not seem rigorously logical.

One intention behind this book is to demonstrate that, when we denigrate our relational knowing and treat the world as if it had only one aspect, we are trying to grasp the world with one hand tied behind our backs. As far as dual creatures like ourselves are concerned, the world is dual and we will only understand it by using both sides of our dual mind. Integrating these, however, requires a careful understanding of their two ways of working.

The idea of a dual mind is, of course, far from new. Many cultures have regarded the human person as fundamentally composite, from the obscure complexities of ancient Egyptian ideas of five interconnected aspects of the person (Dollinger, 2012) to the familiar Christian tradition of body and soul, with "spirit" often distinguished from soul as in the Hebrew system. In many cases such systems have arisen through a need to interpret religious symbolism and practice rather than through philosophical reflection. We shall, however, be concerned particularly with the Western philosophical tradition, and as a background to this I will in the next section give a highly compressed historical sketch of the idea of logic in this tradition, focussing on the words for "logic" and "truth". I will use this to give a more refined classification of the different aspects of our mind.

3.2 The start of the separation: the language of duality

The earliest information on this tradition is to be found in the epic works attributed to Homer, which give us clues as to early Greek thinking. These then need to be supplemented by later philosophical works.

According to Julian Jaynes (1976), the latter part of the Homeric period (6th century BCE) was when the human mind was in a fragile situation, with the two parts, corresponding to the propositional and the relational, standing in an uneasy relation to each other, a moment of transition between separation and co-operation. Ironically, however, the direction of the change seems to have been the reverse of Jaynes' assumption. He supposed that the two mental subsystems were moving from separation towards co-operation, whereas, as McGilchrist (2009, p. 266) has convincingly argued, the direction of travel was precisely the opposite. On McGilchrist's analysis, by the 6th century BCE a greater distance between the subsystems was emerging in Greece, resulting in "an intellectual sense of wonder at the sheer fact of existence, and, consequently, a conviction that our normal ways of construing the world are profoundly mistaken."

The same idea is expressed in Parmenides' writings (5th century BCE). Writings from this period survive to us as fragments, mostly preserved in quotations by later writers, constituting a large, enigmatic, and contested literature. One of Parmenides' fragments (which are expressed as advice given by a goddess to Parmenides) counsels: "let not habit do violence to you on this empirical way, so that you exercise an unseeing eye and a noisy ear and tongue, but decide by discourse *(logos)* the controversial test enjoined by me."[43] In other words, the way in which Parmenides is to seek after truth must proceed empirically, by testing what he discerns; but he must guard against stopping at superficial appearances (immediate experience). Instead he must be guided by logical reasoning to penetrate beyond the senses. This is not, however, an injunction to ditch the senses along with the implicational subsystem and focus solely on the verbal (that was to come much later). The implicational subsystem, the core of consciousness, is still playing a major role.

Another fragment by Parmenides, made famous by Heidegger, starts: "It is necessary to assert *(legein)* and conceive *(noein)*..."[44] He etymologically translates[45] *legein* (the root of *logos* and hence of "logic") as "letting-lie-before-us" and *noein* (the root of *nous* — mind, or thought) as "taking-to-heart". Each of these activities involve both our cognitive subsystems, but in different ways. *Legein* uses the propositional *logos* to set apart a distinct perception for our consideration, without thereby losing its wider implicational relationships, while *noein* connects the perception back into its deeper context. If this interpretation is correct, it would mean that Parmenides' thought was still quite close to the unimpeded to-and-fro of the subsystems that may have held before the Homeric age.

Heidegger's interpretation of the early meaning of *logos* is far from universally accepted, however. The historian of religion Karen Armstrong (2006, pp. 145–46) places the emergence of the concept of *logos* in the first half of the 7th century BCE, when the Greek city-states began to replace their elite fighting corps drawn from the nobility by large armies encompassing all classes. This resulted in a more equal society with a more down to earth way of talking, compared to the language handed down from the epic narratives of Homer's *Iliad* and *Odyssey*. "A farmer who fought next to a nobleman in the phalanx would never see the aristocracy in the same way again. It would not be long before the lower classes demanded that *their* organization—the people's assembly—should take a central role in the government of the city... The new army spoke a different language. *Logos* (dialogue speech) was quite different from the allusive language of Homer and the heroic age."

Armstrong contrasts *logos* with both the poetic speech of the Homeric epics (8th–6th century BCE) and with *rhetoriki*, the art of using speech to sway the listeners' minds. But just as Homeric verse and political oratory are very different sorts of language, so are the languages spoken by "a farmer... in the phalanx" and the founder of logic, Aristotle (4th century BCE). To make matters more complex still, by the time we get to the late 3rd century BCE we find many instances of the word *logos* being used as the translation of the word *dabar* in the Hebrew scriptures, when it is used to mean the creative or active word of God.[46] This echoes Parmenides' (Heidegger's) "letting-lie-before-us"—what is given for contemplation—than it does Armstrong's military speech in the phalanx.

However tangled its details, in terms of concepts the picture that emerges from this process is fairly clear. There is a progressive, if not direct, move from Homer's invoking of the feeling and significance of a scene by means of formalised poetry to a more critical use of language, regarding language as a tool in its own right rather than accepting it as an inseparable part of the human imagination. On the relational side, this too starts to be recognised as a distinct way of knowing. *Logos* and *noein*, respectively, name these two ways. It seems to be the case that *logos* fundamentally draws on the relational and can use the interplay between relational and propositional in different ways. As a result *logos* encompasses the practical speech of warfare, the use of words to exercise power (as in translating *dabar*) and the analytic consideration of a situation (*legein*). All these draw to varying degrees on the relational, while being generated in the propositional. For consistency I will also include rhetoric within *logos*. *Logos* is always at some distance from *noein* – the propositional from the relational – and it is this distancing which accounts both for the strengths and the weaknesses of *logos*.

All these concepts are of little use without the understanding of a process for using them, for which we look to Socrates (5th century BCE). If we can rely on Plato's dramatised descriptions of this philosopher, his delight was to push his discussants to a deeper level by asking them what they meant by the words they used, and then dissecting the response further in order to reveal that the speakers had very little notion of what they were really intending. From this emptiness a path could be built to establish clearer concepts that better grasped the ideas under discussion. The aim of the discussions led by Socrates, as written by Plato, was usually an holistic one, covering grand topics like "love", "beauty", or "government", but it was reached via precise verbal reasoning. This may seem like a strictly formal process well removed from the relational; but this impression is swiftly dispelled on reading the dialogues of Plato. Socrates is presented as a skilful pedagogue who opens up the minds of his hearers and draws out of them a richer understanding of the world than they had realised was possible.

Further in this book we will be looking at the much later development in the seventeenth century of purely formal logics designed in the spirit of mathematics, where the influences of the relational are much weaker. This phase was preceded by a long tradition of what might be called hybrid logic, starting with Aristotle, which used formal rules of deduction and categories of truth but, like Socrates, guided the whole process with input of "common sense" from the implicational. The implementation of a completely formal logic marks a shift in Western ways of knowing as important as that from pre-Homeric to post-Homeric times.

Alongside the reasoning process of *logos* is the vital concept of truth: in Greek *alētheia*. In Homeric works it is mostly used in the straightforward context of speaking the truth, as opposed to a lie (Liddell & Scott, 1996); but Heidegger plausibly argued that underneath this was an implicit meaning that differed from our use of "truth". He noted that the word was a negation of *lanthanein*, meaning to escape notice or be unseen, and that *alētheia* therefore had the sense of uncovering or revealing a concealed reality, consistently with Parmenides' usage. Much later, the famous saying "I am the way, the truth (*alētheia*) and the life" in the Gospel of John indicates a meaning of *alētheia* as revelation.

As *logos* took on a less relational and more propositional flavour, so the relational idea of truth as disclosure was merged with more practical uses in a propositional mode. Karen Armstrong's depiction of logic as serving the needs of warfare suggests a down to earth, factual language whose statements were either true or false in a way that could be verified. "The enemy is camped behind that hill" can be checked by sending a scout to look. This is truth in the sense of *correspondence* with a verifiable state of affairs. The logical dialectic of

Socrates, by contrast, was concerned with pinning down widely embracing abstract ideas by refining the meanings of words so as to build a consistent scheme — a *consistency* sense of truth. It is worth noting that there are at least three different senses of truth at play here: a correspondence sense of truth as disclosure, implied by *noein* and with strong relational links; a more rational, propositional correspondence sense (*legein*); and a consistency sense associated with the Socratic pedagogic technique.

Leaping forward to the era of our quantum theme, we can see that these distinctions play a part in science. In the ideal scientific paradigm, hypothesis formation has an aspect of *noein* — the relational grasp of the essence of a phenomenon — while the development and testing of a model derived from the hypothesis reflects *legein*. If the hypothesis is confirmed by the experimental testing, then it becomes more likely to be "true": at least in the consistency sense of truth, and in classical physics with a likelihood of truth in the correspondence sense.

In quantum theory, however, there was a debate from the start as to whether the results of an experiment can ever be regarded as corresponding to a "reality" in the sense of disclosure. Famously, Einstein argued that this sort of reality was essential to science, while Niels Bohr held that there was no such thing as reality in the quantum world, and all one could expect was consistency.

3.3 The rise of the propositional

The notion of truth either as a purely logical correspondence with a pragmatic verification, or as a manifestation of no more than consistency, is a form of rationality that stems from Aristotle, rather than from his teacher, Plato. The latter, while laying great stress on the supremacy of mathematics and ideas, still retained the *noein* aspect, the aspect of being discerned by the relational mind, as an integral part of reality. Plato straddles a cusp after which the propositional mind was increasingly to dominate, becoming most prominent in physics, which frequently presents itself as uncovering absolute logical correspondence-truth in the form of a mathematical system. This conception of truth and logic is, however, too rigid to solve the inconsistencies in quantum cosmology. To do this, as we shall see later, it has to include consciousness. In the rest of this book we will be exploring a way of restoring another dimension to the pure logic of modern physics, which can form a bridge between this logic and the relational domain in which consciousness can be understood.

There is an important structural point that must be borne in mind in this bridging. Our two subsystems constantly communicate with each other (albeit sometimes not as efficiently as we might like). Since they operate in very different ways, each communication must involve a translation from the form of information that one subsystem uses to the form that the other uses—though we do not at present know what that form is.[47] These hypothetical but clearly necessary translation processes form, as it were, the rigging that keeps Teasdale and Barnard's "interacting cognitive subsystems" on course.

Let us focus on the communication processes between the propositional and relational subsystems. Their two-way interactions make up the core of the human mind, termed by Teasdale and Barnard "the central engine of cognition". When we consider the ways in which the two subsystems process data within themselves, and how they receive translated data from the other half of the central engine, we see that there is actually a *fourfold* division of thinking in this engine, namely:
- how the relational thinks;
- how the propositional thinks;
- what the propositional receives from the relational;
- what the relational receives from the propositional.

Our own conceptual bridges between the subsystems, which enable us think about the workings of this engine of cognition, have to take into account parts of this fourfold division. The task of building these bridges will draw on the insights of Kant and those of spiritual traditions, noted in chapter 1, as well as Foucault's ideas which draw attention to the processes of knowing rather than to an absolute concept of knowledge or truth. The central theme of this book, however, will concern the possibility of placing side by side, in interaction, an absolute Newtonian concept of truth alongside a dynamic process of knowing, doing, and being. This way of thinking, moreover, has to be compatible with a range of alternative views of the world. Until recently this would have been impossible because these two approaches to knowing have drifted so far apart. Now, however, recent developments in quantum logic have directed attention to forms of logic that represent (albeit at a formal level) the ways of knowing of our relational mind. After the millennia in which they have drifted apart, the needs of quantum theory are starting to bring them together, to the benefit both of quantum theory and of our understanding of the perceived world.

Later in this book we will explore how the propositional ways of knowing can be brought into a more explicit unity through representing the relational to itself by the use of non-standard logics.

3.4 Logic and mind

We return to our chronological sketch at the point where Plato presents a two-pronged attack on the mystery of existence. The figure of Socrates combines the training of thought into a consistent system (consistency being one criterion for truth) while at the same time truth is seen as a revelation of a reality lying beyond or behind the uncertain features of everyday appearance.

This balanced approach was followed up by Aristotle who combined (among his numerous abilities) the curiosity of a true scientist in his examination of natural phenomena with a codification of logic in two books of

Analytics. The latter examined what he claimed were all possible patterns of argument, classifying them into those that were *valid* (always reaching true conclusions if given true premises) and those which were not. While the investigative spirit of his proto-science had little impact, the "syllogisms" setting out in ideal form the valid structures for reasoning, formed a basis for logic which endured, with minor changes, for the next 1400 years.

Aristotle's work on logic was revolutionary because of its formality. The "rhetoric" which had preceded it was an artistic skill, a process of engaging the minds of the hearers so as to sway them to your intentions. Logic, by contrast, was about following rules, a process whose validity was supposed to be incontestable. In this spirit Leibniz was to write, some 2000 years later, "I am therefore working towards the production of a method which will always be able, for every argument, to cast people's thinking into the form of calculations, so that there will be no need, as now, to raise a fuss, but one could say to another, 'calculemus' [let us calculate]."[48] It was a process dominated by the left hemisphere/propositional subsystem.

This was the logic that became the foundation of modern science, as can be seen both in the structure of scientific papers and in the concept of "laws of nature". Papers strive to be logically correct in all their details and to set out precisely their initial assumptions and their sources. Newton in his revolutionary writings asserted the existence of absolute "laws" governing the universe that give a warrant for such a process. Unlike the laws made by the rulers of societies, these are "laws which never shall be broken",[49] suggestive of an ideal logic that rules the universe. So it would seem that logic, the discipline developed in order to improve human decision making, turned out to be something rather different: namely the foundation structure of the universe.

This is reflected in, for example, the work of Jean Piaget, the child psychologist who was the first to investigate and codify the development in young children of their reasoning about the world. He described this development in terms of the "growth of logic in the child" (Inhelder & Piaget, 1964), referring to the process whereby, for example, the child acquired and learned to use concepts such as the constancy of the volume of the liquid in a glass when it was transferred to a glass of a different shape. Here "logic" is a form of epistemology, of discovering the nature of the world through developing appropriate reasoning (Piaget & Grize, 1972). Piaget regarded human development as the progressive learning of a mental logic that matched the logic of the external world.

Today most scientists would argue that, at least as far as classical (pre-quantum) science is concerned, the world turns out to be logical (in Aristotle's sense), as an empirical finding. If this were so, one could then take Piaget's argument further, from the growth of logic in an individual to its growth in human beings as a species. It is then likely that we humans evolved ways of decision making that fitted with the sort of universe that we lived in. An empirically rational universe is one in which the world of experience will exhibit many regularities (albeit often concealed by the complexity of our ecosystem) and thus it is no coincidence that, in refining our own decision making, we should move towards rules more like those governing the universe as a result of Darwinian evolution or "social evolution".

Thus it would seem that the dictum of Parmenides (or perhaps only of Heidegger!) at the start of this section, urging a two-pronged grasp of the world, has fallen by the wayside, in favour of a single-logic approach. But if we truly wish to understand the world and ourselves, then our relational knowing must once more be acknowledged: not only as an essential part of being human, but also as an essential part of physics, required in order to formulate a credible role for consciousness in quantum theory. The problem with this, however, is that the logical structure used in physics has moved so far away from Parmenides' *noein* that it is hard to see how they can be reconnected.

I suggest that the solution to this dilemma lies in the concept of modelling. Though the Aristotelian logic of science cannot directly grasp the very different processes of the relational subsystem, what it can do and what it does in the majority of its areas of application, is to model it.

A model represents some aspects of the phenomenon that are of current interest and ignores others that are not. Modelling in this technical sense is closely parallel to its more colloquial sense of, for example, the construction of a small wooden replica of a large metal ship. The model is faithful to the original regarding many important aspects, such as (in the case of the ship) the relative sizes of the main parts of the object. For other aspects there may be an adequate way of translating those pertaining to the model into those pertaining to the original. For example, the speed of the ship through the water might be given reasonably closely by applying a mathematical transformation which related the speed of the ship in response to a particular driving force to the speed of the model in response to an appropriately transformed driving force. Other aspects, however, such as the material used, details of equipment, and so on, would be quite different. The point is that the model can be constructed quickly and easily, and useful information can be gained from it, despite the vastly greater complexity of the original.

In mathematics the use of the word "modelling" becomes generalised in a way that can be baffling for those unfamiliar with the idea. A model of, for example, an industrial plant for producing synthetic fibres (Fitt *et al.*, 2002) could consist entirely of a set of equations rather than a physical device. The equations would be so designed that, when one feeds into them numerical specifications of the inputs to the real plant (for example specifications of the composition and initial temperature of the plastic material) then the formulae can predict the optimum rate that should be supplied for moving the thread through the plant, the quality of product, and similar factors. Such a model replaces a physical entity by a conceptual entity, but the possibility of translation between the two remains.

Fortunately there are now several systems that can provide ideas for models of the relational subsystem, even though this was not their original purpose. The ones most relevant to this task will be drawn from the more exotic areas of quantum theory; but as an initial example I will use the psychological case of "symmetric logic" introduced by Ignacio Matte Blanco, a psychoanalyst, in attempting to understand the operation of the Freudian unconscious.

Matte Blanco was seeking to use the statements made by patients in analysis in order to understand unconscious processes, and he proposed that this could be done by regarding them *as if* they were arising in part from an alternative sort of logic, which he called symmetric logic. The "as if" is important here. The unconscious is presumed to operate in a way that cannot be called "logic" in the usual sense; but the propositional mind can get an understanding of the unconscious in its own terms by using symmetric logic as a model. By using this logical system Matte Blanco obtained a provisional understanding of the structural processes going on in analysis. Much of the approach that follows later in this book—such as the way in which the propositional mind makes sense of the relational mind—is inspired by Matte Blanco's work.

His first principle is that every individual thing is treated by the unconscious as belonging to nested wider classes that provide a context for the logic.[50] The most important idea in Matte Blanco's account, expressed as his second principle, then concerns *relations* within a particular context. A relation can hold between two similar things, as for instance in the case of the relationship "John is the son of Mary", or it can hold between an individual and a property, as in "John is kind". Matte Blanco's second and central principle is then that all such relationships are equivalent to their converse: that is, from the above examples it follows, for the unconscious, that "Mary is the [daughter] of John" or that "[kindness] is John" — i.e. John is the quintessence of kindness.[51]

At a first reading this principle sounds ridiculous, and indeed Matte Blanco's framing of the idea within conventional mathematical logic seems strained. The point is, however, that this logic has two distinctive features:
- It works through *association* rather than propositions in the usual sense; and
- It is *unquantified*. Properties cannot hold to varying degrees. It is a matter of all or nothing (or both!)

John and Mary are associated within the context of progeny; John and kindness are associated and kindness is absolute. This is so different from normal logic that it might seem absurd. This is, however, an account of how the essentially non-logical relational mind appears to the propositional mind. The latter can then regard it as an alternative logic that serves as a model of the relational. In modelling, the question is not "is this realistic?" but "is this a coherent system and is it fruitful: does it give an insight into the area under investigation?"

Another key proposal in his system is that "p and not-p are identical" (Matte Blanco, 1998, p. 40). This clearly denies one of the bastions of classical logic, namely the "principle of non-contradiction" which asserts that "p" and "not-p" cannot both be true at the same time. In parallel with this he concludes, more fundamentally, that "there is no negation" (*ibid.*, p. 47) — but subsequently he has no qualms about using "not" and the equivalent symbol "~" in what follows! The overarching point here is the fact that the propositional subsystem thrives on getting right the distinctions between various uses of "negation",[52] while the relational subsystem by its very nature blurs and aggregates any precise dichotomies.

This raises the whole question of paradox, which has often been associated with the transcendent — perhaps most famously by Nicolas of Cusa[53] who refers to the "coincidence of contradictories". The role of context is vital here (it is perhaps the most important theme in this book, and is considered in the next section).

In some contexts the individual can stand for a whole class of which it is a part. Thus, a dream featuring a startling shade of *red* might, from a broader perspective, be indicating the more general property of *colour*, and from this perspective *red* and *green* might be "identical" (i.e. functionally equivalent). Following on from this, Matte Blanco argues that for a given proposition p there is always a context within which p and *not-p* are identical (see [e. 52]).

Importantly, symmetric logic is never manifested on its own, but always in conjunction with the ordinary (asymmetric) logic that dominates the propositional mind. Matte Blanco calls this combination "bilogic". It is this that prevails in our thinking: we virtually never have either form of logic manifested on its own. In bilogic the symmetric part steers dynamically from one context to the next, drawing in associated ideas that might be relevant at each stage, while the asymmetric part analyses the result and filters out the more outrageous parts. Language itself is rooted in bilogic rather than asymmetric logic, as has been argued by Delal (1998), even though language is preeminently a left hemisphere activity.

Coherence is not a problem: a relationship is a well-defined propositional structure and symmetrical relationships can be constructed consistently, even though there are problems with Matte Blanco's attempt to integrate it into set theory. Matte Blanco does not, in fact, give any adequate account[54] of what sort of logical rules are to be applied to his system — but it turns out that the system will work, mathematically speaking, with a few straightforward alterations of the normal rules of logic (Bomford, 1999; Clarke, 2010). I hope that the fruitfulness of modelling such as this will become progressively more convincing in the course of this book!

One might ask what evidence is there for the extraordinary logic that Matte Blanco produces? My response to this would have to be, there is very little evidence. Posing the question in this way, however, is to misunderstand what Matte Blanco did. He listened to his psychiatric clients and found utterances only loosely and idiosyncratically connected, but having a sort of regularity of their own. Because of his enthusiasm for the work of Russell and Whitehead in mathematics he forced the structure of these utterances into the formalism of mathematical set theory.

I will not be relying explicitly on Matte Blanco's model in this book, but will be taking from it the idea of a logic of statements connected not by the detailed logic of verbal thinking (as used by the propositional mind) but only by a simpler process that seems to be a common core for both the relational and propositional minds, namely context dependent association.

3.5 Truth and context

In the previous section we considered the use of logic to model how systems within the mind (such as Freud's "unconscious" or Teasdale's relational system) actually implemented the process of reasoning, even though we might be suspicious of the correctness of the conclusions they came up with. The conventional way of looking at logic, by contrast, is as a means of attaining truth; of getting the reasoning correct. Aristotle expounded his system of syllogisms—patterns for correct reasoning—so that teachers and statesmen could form correct conclusions, provided they started from correct premises (a vital qualification!) This, however, requires us to be clear as to what truth is, and, as Oscar Wilde reminds us, truth is "rarely pure and never simple".

Before the modern era (but after the pre-Aristotelian period surveyed in section 3.2) it was assumed that truth was a matter of correspondence with the world and that the sole aim of logic was to grasp it as securely as possible. The subsequent history of logic had been an extension of Aristotle's ideas regarding syllogisms without any alteration of their basic form. Even in Aristotle and his mediaeval followers, however, there was a tacit recognition that the black and white distinction between "true" and "false" was an oversimplification.

Following Kant's "Copernican shift"[55] of viewpoint from the known to the knower, the notion of truth has become contested and its importance downgraded. In place of an absolute truth "out there" we need to consider the quality and coherence of the various ways of knowing in operation "down here". Truth loses its status as an eternal certainty and it is replaced by a fluid and evolving consensus between various ways of knowing. Truth is a river, not a rock.

Scientists will not be surprised by this. A famous unwritten paper by Charles Misner[56] has as its theme the idea that absolute truth is to be found only in theories that have been refuted; for, once this has occurred for some theory, the bounds of the domain within which it is valid are known and statements about truth and error can now be made with more certainty.

More specifically, one could raise questions about the relation between truth and knowledge: does it make sense to talk about the truth or falsity of a statement if there is no possible way of discovering this without in the process altering the situation? This seems to be what is happening in quantum theory.

The inclusion of the dimension of time raises further complications. To quote an example studied by Aristotle, consider the statement "The sea battle tomorrow will be won by us." Is this a statement which can in principle be today either true or false (though we do not know which); or does it have some intermediate status today, which will turn into truth or falsity tomorrow? These puzzles led in the 20th century to the emergence of three-valued logics (using, for instance, "true", "false", and "indeterminate"), modal logics using the additional qualities of "necessity" and "possibility", and tensed logics where time entered the formalism explicitly. Usually more than one of these is used together within the same system.

The development most of interest in this book is the idea of *context dependent logic* which, to some extent, brings together the varieties of logic just mentioned. Only in mathematics is a statement absolutely true or absolutely false:[57] when it comes to a statement in a natural language, the context is essential for understanding the statement and deciding on its validity.

To understand what is meant by context dependent logic, consider the process of receiving an ordinary remark, such as "Miggy is on the mat." This process involves three levels. First there is a *sentence*: an actual sequence of words, spoken or written. Then, second, there is the meaning of the sentence, the *statement* that it is making, which is highly dependent on the *context* in which it is uttered or written. If we are in the house of someone who owns a cat called Miggy, who is wont to sit on a particular mat, and the sentence is uttered at some particular time, then we will instantly grasp its particular meaning in this context. If, on the other hand, Miggy is the wife of my friend who utters the sentence, after explaining that she has had an argument with her employer, then we will grasp a quite different meaning: the sentence is the same, but it will be making a different statement.

The third stage, if we are interested in the truth of the statement, will be its *validation*, comparing the statement with either "Reality" or with a currently accepted pragmatic world-view. In the first context for the Miggy sentence, validation simply involves going and looking on the cat's preferred mat. In the second context, it might depend on individual interpretations: what I might regard as a serious reprimand warranting the phrase "on the mat" might be regarded by Miggy herself as no more than casual disagreement. Here the question of context becomes very individual and flexible.

In order to handle these levels of truth, several authors had considered formal logical systems (i.e. versions of mathematical logic) in which the context is represented explicitly in the formalism used. The monumental work of Goddard and Routley (1973) does this by making the sentence/statement separation just exemplified: between a *sentence,* in the ordinary sense of a certain collection of words in a natural language (as opposed to a formal mathematical "language"), and a *statement* which is the *significance* of the sentence. The *context* is then what determines the conversion of a sentence into a statement. Goddard and Routley were particularly interested in using the notion of context to clarify the logical problem of handling apparently meaningless sentences, such as "Virtue is not triangular" (Haack, 1978) or the delightful "Colorless green ideas sleep furiously" (Chomsky, 1957).

These are examples of sentences for which there is supposedly no context in which they have significance. The trouble is that it is hard to imagine any sentence that is totally meaningless, without its ceasing to be a sentence. Examples such as those just quoted often have a pronounced surreal aura to them, from which some sort of meaning can be extracted within a suitably ingenious context. What can be said, however, is that in most contexts these sentences do not yield a statement. By drawing attention to context the situation becomes clearer.

The Kantian shift from the known to the knower, from reality to ways of knowing, fits well with an emphasis on context — whether it be the context of a particular individual knower or a social context with a characteristic way of knowing (see §3.1). Both the propositional and the relational subsystems have a role in determining this context, with the relational particularly involved in determining the most vital but subtle aspects of the context. When it comes to considering quantum theory the propositional mind is completely dominant, but here, too, context is vital: it is the situation—usually specified as a particular sort of measuring apparatus in a physics laboratory—which determines which quantities of a physical system become available for measurement. Later we will be examining the particular case of the highly context dependent *topos logic* in order to see how it can model the context dependence of at least some aspects of our mind.

In all these approaches to logic, we need still to recall that they are in essence propositional. Logic is different from Parmenides' "*legein*" of §3.2 . The latter is a relationship, the taking of a stance in relation to the world before you, as you assert verbally some aspect of this encounter. Its context is your creation, not merely a position that you passively occupy. Both you and the other are altered in this relationship. None of this is reflected in the contextual and similar logics that we have just discussed, which all fit within the static givenness of mathematics.[58] It is this latter, propositional form of logic that we will be considering in the next chapter.

Synopsis

- Knowledge is not a neutral commodity, but the product of acts of human knowing. The nature of knowing is shaped by the division of the mind into propositional and relational, and by the (sub-)cultures to which the knower belongs.
- The culturally dominant way of knowing in the West arises from the drifting apart of the propositional and relational aspects of the mind, starting in late classical Greek culture.

- The duality of mind leads to a fourfold division of the way in which mind reflects on itself. Modelling is a way in which the propositional can understand the relational.
- Forms of context dependent logic seem the most effective way of modelling the relational.

Four

The Reinvention of Quantum Logic

This chapter summarises developments in the logic of quantum theory which have paralleled those in the logic of mind. It focusses on two logical systems: quantum logic developed in 1936 and topos logic developed between 1998 and 2011.

4.1 Birkhoff-von Neumann logic

The idea that quantum theory had its own form of logic was initiated by Birkhoff and von Neumann (1936), but their work mainly had the effect of convincing physicists and logicians that the idea was not very useful. The steady expansion in the scope and variety of logic over the past 60 years, however, stimulated increasing interest in applying similar ideas to the logic of quantum theory (see, for example, the surveys by Beltrametti, 1981; and Garden, 1983). In 1998 this process took a decisive turn with a series of papers by Chris Isham and Jeremy Butterfield (1998) that could radically transform thinking about quantum theory.

Quantum theory, like most of physics, is based on measurements. We usually think of measurements as processes for determining numbers (representing positions, temperatures, and so on) and we think of numbers as being strung out as points on a line—a way of thinking that is useful in applying mathematics to the measuring process. But real measurements are always carried out with particular solid machines with a limited accuracy (however small its errors might be). Beyond this level of accuracy it does not make sense to distinguish between one measured value and another close value. In such a case it is more appropriate (though not necessarily more convenient) to record a result like "the position of this particle is between 10 mm and 11 mm from the wall." So for some purposes it is more realistic to think of a measurement not as yielding a continuously varying mathematical number, but as yielding one of a finite of possible value-ranges. This can in turn be represented as a series of yes-or-no tests ("is it between 1 mm and 2 mm?", "is it between 2 mm and 3 mm?, etc.) one for each of these values. In this way measurements can be reduced to the much simpler case of testing the truth or falsity of a series of true or false statements (e.g. "it is between 1 mm and 2 mm"). Such true-or-false statements are known as *propositions*. They play a vital role when it comes to philosophising about quantum theory.

Propositions are the stuff of logic, which is essentially about formulating procedures for combining simple propositions into more complex ones (e.g. "the particle is at 15–16 mm *or* it is at 16–17 mm") and determining the truth of complex propositions given the truth of elementary ones. This is essentially what was achieved by Aristotle's system of syllogisms. As we have already noted, however, the rules seem to be different in quantum theory: in particular, we have noted that the Kochen-Specker theorem implies that, under classical logic, a quantum system cannot be said to possess, at a given time, values of all the quantities for which one might perform measurements, while respecting any fixed relationships between the measurements. Since a measurement can always be constructed from propositions of a form like "the position of the particle in mm lies between 1 and 2", this is equivalent to the more tractable result that it is impossible, within standard logic, to assign a truth-value (true or false) to every *proposition* (a measurement with a yes/no outcome) about the system. This suggests (if you are a mathematician taking little notice of the real world around you) that we might try using some alternative logic which handles propositions differently from classical logic.

In fact, such an alternative logic, in a purely formal and left-hemisphere sense of 'logic', is already provided by the mathematical structure of quantum states (sections 2.2 and 2.6) as an elaborated geometry, in which a proposition is represented as a plane formed from all the quantum states for which the proposition is true. Then logical constructions can be naturally turned into geometrical constructions, and vice versa.[59] The mathematicians Garrett Birkhoff and John von Neumann (Birkhoff, 1936) built a logic based on this correspondence between geometrical objects and propositions. The resulting "BvN logic" set the pattern for many subsequent variations.

At one level the logic is successful. It does escape from the Kochen-Specker theorem[60] in the sense that BvN logic is weaker than standard logic and so this theorem cannot be proved using BvN logic. This logic is not concerned with the actual state of affairs that can be imputed to a quantum system, but with the specification of a particular measurement that can be carried out, with a result that will either confirm or deny some proposition. But this seems to be evading precisely the aspect of quantum theory which one wants to investigate, namely "what is going on out there?"

The key difference between BvN logic and conventional logic lies in the rules — termed "distributive laws" — for combining propositions using "and" and "or". Chris Isham (2006) has famously illustrated this with the example of the question, asked by a waiter in a restaurant, "Would you like eggs and sausage or bacon?" In ordinary logic we will automatically see this as equivalent to "Would you like eggs and sausage or would you like eggs and bacon?" More concisely, using letters to stand for propositions (well, questions in this case) like "Would you like eggs" the distributive law being used here is

A **and** (*B* **or** *C*) **is equivalent to** (*A* **and** *B*) **or** (*A* **and** *C*).

Isham points out that it would be very odd if, after being asked "Would you like eggs and sausage or bacon?" you requested eggs and sausage, and were informed that neither eggs and sausage nor eggs and bacon were available. He argued convincingly that this law was so fundamental to what one means by "logic" that it is worth looking for a form of quantum logic that is not so unreasonably contrary to what one normally thinks of as logic. The question is, what is reasonable in logic, and what does one really want to use logic for?

The problem with logical laws, like this distributive law, is that they are promulgated as timeless realities manipulating propositions that can be pinned down with complete precision. This is fine for propositions like "2 + 2 = 4" (though even this might be queried by some), but in real life things are much more fluid than that. In the case of the breakfast menu just cited, the terms are probably sufficiently definite to pin down what is meant. However, "sausage or bacon" might refer to a concoction of processed bacon that cannot with honesty be described as either sausage or bacon. Logic is not necessarily clearcut in ordinary life because life is too complex, and it is not applicable in quantum theory because the situation is fundamentally different from ordinary life. We need to rethink what we mean by logic and what are its laws, and in the process we will find deeper connections between physics and life.

When it comes to the logic of quantum theory, the obstacle to a conventional logic is the uncertainty principle (§2.1). According to this, there are always certain propositions A and B for which measuring the value of a quantity A is likely to generate uncertainty in some other variable B, and verse versa. In such a case the truth or falsity of *A* and *B* cannot be determined simultaneously and so no prediction can be made about measuring "*A* and *B*". As a result, it is an open question whether statements like "both *A* and *B* are true" are meaningful propositions or not. If propositions cannot, at a fundamental level, be *determined* simultaneously, can such propositions *have* a condition of truth or falsity independently of their measurement? If ones tries to modify logic to allow uncertain situations like mashed bacon or quantum uncertainty, then one policy might be to introduce, in addition to 'true' and 'false', a third logical value of "undetermined", as has been tried by several authors (Garden, 1983). This, however, may merely cover up the problems, whereas the real interest lies in understanding the different reasons for the lack of determination.

As we have seen, Birkhoff and von Neumann took a different course. They decided that making a correspondence between aspects of the geometry of quantum space and aspects of logic could be used to get round the ambiguity of logical statements in quantum theory, proposing that "*A* and *B*" should be given a purely geometrical definition,[61] even in cases when this is not a measurable proposition. The result of this is to weaken the scope of logical argument, in the sense that fewer propositions can be logically proved to be definitely true or false.

4.2 Context and degrees of truth

The decisive step taken by Isham in 1998 was to introduce into quantum theory a form of context dependent logic, ultimately based on topos theory,[62] in which the context was freely variable. This naturally gave rise to a more general notion of truth: truth became "elastic", with many values between true and false. This was quite different from alternative approaches that merely used "true", "false", and "undecided". Where BvN logic moved away from standard logic towards pure geometry, Isham's approach moved towards the flexible way in which logic operates in everyday life, while still representing it through rigorous mathematics.

A quite different approach was used in the earlier context logic of Routley (§3.5), which was based on sentences and contexts that varied independently of each other which together produced a "significance". The significance then was assigned a value of true or false as usual. In contrast, the structures described by Isham and his collaborators deal with logical packages of "statement + elastic-truth" which vary from one context to another. Isham presents a series of papers that develop a variety of different implementations of the idea, drawing progressively more from constructions that are natural in topos theory. I will sketch here some of the basic ideas in one of the simplest papers (Isham, 2006), which also has the advantage of being expressed in terms similar to those used by BvN logic, while also making use of the way in which measurements are expressed in quantum theory.

The most important idea is that of a "window on reality" analogous to the windows we have already encountered from Mary Midgley[e. 19] and in the details of the Kochen-Specker theorem.[e. 60] In the case of this paper, each measurable quantity (on some fixed given system) — for instance "energy" or "speed of rotation" — defines a window, a way of looking at the system in question. Actual measurements of a quantity involve propositions such as "the energy is between 2 joules and 3 joules", and geometrically the proposition corresponds to a projection in quantum space: an operation that collapses the space of quantum states down onto a smaller space of states that are, in this particular context, "true". (This makes contact with BvN logic which is based on the geometry of quantum space.) Any of the propositions *within a given window* can be determined simultaneously without interfering with each other, so they satisfy the rules of ordinary logic.

While there are mathematical similarities with BvN logic, this scheme has the crucial addition of *context*. A particular projection might belong to two different windows which set it within two different contexts. For instance, one window might deal with energy and the projection might correspond to "the energy is between 2 joules and 3 joules", while another window might deal with rotation and the same projection correspond to "the speed of rotation is between 100 rps and 200 rps." A context is interpreted operationally as a particular sort of measurement on the system, and represented mathematically as a particular transformation in quantum space: a correspondence between meaning and mathematics runs through the whole structure.[63]

What makes this system work is the notion of *coarse graining*. One window W is said to be a coarse graining of another window A if any proposition w in W can be expressed as

$$w = a \text{ or } b \text{ or } c \text{ or } \ldots$$

where $a, b, c, \ldots$ are propositions in A. In this case w can be called a coarse-grading of a (or of b, etc.) with respect to W. In other words, the propositions of context W describe things in broad-brush terms and conversely the propositions in context A are more refined sub-divisions of propositions in context W. It is this that enables one to define a flexible notion of truth: the **truth-value** of a proposition a in A is a specification of the all the coarse-grainings W of A in which the coarse-grading of a with respect to W is (genuinely) true. So the truth-value of a is not a straight yes or no, or even a quantified "80% yes", but a statement of how you have to water down a in order that the result be true. As a result, the notion of "truth" obeys different rules from those of conventional logic. In particular, there is no simple negation: since there are gradations of truth the construction "not true" is not a useful operation.

4.3 Superposition

This logic, with its incompatible windows on reality and flexible concepts of truth, can be related to a more basic aspect of quantum theory that physicists have had to live with since the start of the subject, namely the phenomenon of superposition. We have already briefly noted[p. 42] how entanglement is represented mathematically by an expression such as $e \otimes P + f \otimes Q$. Here the multiplication "$\otimes$" sign represents the combination of two different systems into a single, more complex, complex system. The addition "+" sign[e. 27] denotes a different sort of combination in which two states of the same system are brought together into a new state that is neither one nor the other. If one makes observations on the state $e + f$, say, to determine whether the system is one state or the other, then half the time the result will be "e" and half the time it will be "f". A situation like this is called a *superposition* of e and f. Superpositions make alternative windows possible: if one compares two different windows, there will be definite states in one window that only appear in superpositions in the other window.

Measurements that are incompatible because of Heisenberg's uncertainty principle are related by superpositions. A state that has a definite value for one measurement will be a superposition of definite states for another measurement.

Synopsis

This work opens up a whole new area of possibility for interpreting quantum theory, and its fruits have yet to develop. I will end this section with a condensed survey of its implications in the context of this book.

- The structures of logic and quantum theory that are introduced in this sort of logic are not arbitrary, but are co-ordinated by the requirement that the system should be a topos.
- The linked use of degrees of truth and context dependence introduces into physics a logical structure that is closer to human thought processes and ways of knowing than is the logic of classical physics or BvN logic.

- The concept of "windows on reality" is integrated into the system, suggesting ways of placing it within a wider picture that includes the consciousness of multiple beings.[64]
- The basic interpretational problem of how a world with specific structures emerges from a homogeneous state of quantum cosmology is still not solved.[e, 64]

Five

What Does Consciousness Do?

There are three immediate possible answers to this question.
- *It collapses the quantum state (or the equivalent of this in other interpretations of quantum theory)*
- *It organises the higher-level functions of the brain*
- *It does nothing, being merely a by-product of brain function.*

All these possibilities, however, are open to severe criticism.

There is also a different kind of answer, namely that consciousness delivers a real universe.

5.1 Where the (quantum) buck stops

In §2.5,[p. 38] we examined Fritz London and Edmund Bauer's account (1939) of the chain of interactions involved in measurement, from the movement of a particle in an experimental chamber, to a detector, perhaps then to a recording device, and finally to a human observer. (Later in this chapter[p. 115] we will consider a refinement of this last step into the registration of what has happened by sensory organs and the parts of the brain that process their signals, followed by action in the seat of consciousness.)

The first steps in this chain had already been described by von Neumann (1932). London and Bauer took the additional step to the observer who, through her capacity to introspect—that is, to observe her own observing—closed off a chain of interactions which might have continued indefinitely. Quite how self-observation achieves this is left vague by them. Here I will explore the possibility that the buck actually stops at the observer's seat of consciousness. It is possible for it to stop here because at this point the information moves from the abstract world of physics and enters the authentic world of experience. For, however accurately verified the physics may be, it is always at one remove from the actual world which is, as Kant taught us, the observed world.

To understand London and Bauer's scenario whereby consciousness might terminate the chain of effects in a measurement, suppose that the quantum state of the particle in the laboratory apparatus is in a superposition[e. 30, p. 98] of two quantum states which, at the end of the chain of effects, would be consciously experienced in two quite different ways. This quantum state then evolves under the direction of the part of the Hamiltonian that determines the development between one stage and the next. Each stage of the chain brings about the entanglement of the state with a further layer. The superposition is preserved at each stage of the transmission of the quantum state, so that the seat of consciousness enters a state that is also a superposition. But a superposition of two states is not something that can normally be conceived in our consciousness: something "has to give".

What happens at this point of observation depends on the different interpretations of quantum theory sketched in §2.5 and the succeeding sections: collapse, splitting, or histories — as follows.

a. Under the conventional interpretations one possibility or the other of the two superposed states is experienced. The quantum state of the universe collapses as a result of selection by consciousness so as to conform to the state that is being experienced.
b. Under Everett's "splitting" interpretation the universe splits into many branches with a different outcome experienced in each.

c. In the generalised histories interpretation (§2.9), the content of this conscious moment is included in a domain that is part of a generalised history. From this, the Hamiltonian extracts a probability of the history as a whole, depending on what outcomes appear from each domain. The underlying guiding quantum state of the universe continues in its unchanged symmetrical state. The co-ordination built into the histories interpretation ensures consistency between what different observers are seeing.

Note that in (a) and (c) the quantum state is reduced to a definite outcome, either by an alteration in the state of the universe or by recording an outcome in a definitive history, while in (b) both outcomes remain, but in different universes corresponding to the splitting. In this splitting version the observer herself is split into an equivalent number of copies, each of whom is unaware of this cosmic catastrophe! But since there is no way of discerning that the other copies exist, this interpretation is equivalent to the collapse interpretation: replacing "collapsing" by "splitting" makes no difference to what we observe or to the physics: it simply proposes a different story for the same facts.

5.2 The operation of consciousness

Let us now focus in more detail on the role of consciousness in this picture, the role of selecting "my world" out of a quantum soup of possibility. We can pick up the historical account from the point when, following the sophisticated mathematical formalism of von Neumann (1955 [1932]), London and Bauer (1983 [1939])[p. 38] adopted a simplified formalism and explicitly discussed the role of consciousness. These two contributions represent what are now "mainstream" approaches based on the scenario described in the previous section. The fundamental act for quantum theory is an "observation". This takes place through two steps: an "automatic" step governed by the

Hamiltonian (called by von Neumann "process 2", even though it comes first) followed by a separate process (von Neumann's "process 1") which according to London and Bauer involves consciousness.

Von Neumann treats the combination system + apparatus as having a mixed (statistical but non-classical) state from the start, in recognition of the fact that we never have a complete microscopic knowledge of the apparatus: the pure state is an idealisation, only achievable in the exceptional conditions of a laboratory apparatus. London and Bauer, on the other hand, focus for simplicity on the case of a pure state. We now know that the system + apparatus necessarily must be treated as having a mixed state because it is entangled with the environment, which results in an essentially classical statistical state (decoherence). This gives rise to the preferential selection and displaying of aspects of the system as viewed through one particular "window", depending on the design of the experiment. When it comes to applying this argument to part of the brain, as we shall consider later, these aspects need to be modified.

When a human observer is also included in the experiment, they can be regarded as an extension of the "apparatus" as far as process 2 is concerned. In addition, however, the ingredient of consciousness brings about the second process (process 1!) in which there is a "collapse" to a different state. Here we strike the fundamental problem with the whole project of completing quantum theory through consciousness: what exactly is going on in "process 1"?

Von Neumann, working with a statistical state, could give an answer that was straightforward, but inadequate. No particular mechanism was suggested, but empirically what happened was that the quantum state, with its possibility for interference, was replaced by a classical statistical state constructed by applying to the state (including the brain) a simple mathematical operation based on the mathematical representation of the observation involved. This had two drawbacks that could have been apparent at the time. The first was that it duplicated the observation process, which was first carried out in the apparatus, and then (though this was only implicit in his writing) repeated in the brain. The second was that it did not yield a definite outcome. The world and the observer's perception were still spread over the whole range of possibilities. At a later date the third drawback emerged, when it was realised that von Neumann's statistical mixed state was already achieved through process 2, but by means of interaction with the environment and consequent decoherence.

London and Bauer, however, recognised that the observer is conscious of one particular result, so that the "collapse" necessarily goes further and results in a single observed outcome, but they could produce no clear account of how consciousness could do it. These points are summarised in the table below.

London & Bauer	von Neumann	Process no.
Pure state	Mixed state	start
Recording		2
Collapse to outcome	Collapse to classical mixed state	1

It is worth noting that in the Bauer/von Neumann approach the action of the seat of consciousness is inherently quantum mechanical (as will be discussed in the next chapter). In the language of von Neumann, consciousness is continually performing process 1. Consequently the particular case of an experiment in quantum physics is rather anomalous, in that the characteristics of a measurement are duplicated. First there is the physical measurement which at least reduces the state to a mixture appropriate to a particular window; then there is the quantum process of the seat of consciousness which performs its own observation.

The "state" here is a *local state*,[p. 44] which, if we are taking into account the entanglement of a state with its environment—even its immediate environment—must be regarded as a mixed state. The distinction between "pure" and "mixed" is often a source of confusion, particularly since there is no tangible concept of "reality" in quantum theory. So in classical statistics we may describe a die that has just been thrown as being in a mixed state, but we know that "really" it has a perfectly definite classical state. In this case the "mixed state" designation refers to our information, while the "classical state" refers to "reality". London and Bauer claim, at one point, that the same can be said of quantum theory, and that "collapse" is similarly a change in information; but the Kochen-Specker theorem shows that there is more to quantum theory than this, and that "reality" is more complex.

A similar thinking seems to be implicitly present in von Neumann's approach, when he stops at the "mixed state" without analysing how a definite outcome appears, assuming that the situation is the same as that of the thrown die. The quantum mixed state arising from decoherence is also the result of our lack of information—in this case, about the environmental interaction—but if we had the information, it would take us to a global state where different outcomes were superposed, not to a classical state. The basic problem of getting to a single outcome is being covered up. Where the situation is one of a laboratory experiment, in which the structure of the recording part of the apparatus singles out a particular "window" (Zurek, 1981), von Neumann's "collapse"[65] is actually just a simulation of what happens in decoherence, which does not bring one any closer to an actual outcome. This need not happen, however, in the case of quantum processes taking place in a small seat of consciousness in the brain.

When we are considering the role of consciousness in situations other than a laboratory, the situation is somewhat different, though the same problems arise. In particular, when we are directly considering the role of consciousness on quantum processes in the brain, then it may be that the "seat" of consciousness is physically small: on a scale intermediate between that of atoms or subatomic particles and that of massive objects whose behaviour is essentially Newtonian. In such a case the full scope of decoherence need not take place (see p. 44 for environmental decoherence and p. 56 for the second decoherence process). Small components of the seat of consciousness are used by Hameroff and Penrose (1996) and by Stapp in the models described below.

These ideas take us nearer to understanding how consciousness might be modelled in quantum mechanical terms. Consciousness must do something more than just adding one more layer to the sequence of particles–measurement–recording, which can never produce a single outcome. In general the seat of consciousness will not be concerned with processing the result of an external "measurement", the scenario that concerns physicists, but with understanding what is going on in the brain. A seat with this intermediate size, open both to quantum effects and to a limited amount of decoherence in its local state p. 44 is a possible environment for a process that is distinct from measurement, which reflects — as far as is possible at the propositional level — some aspects of consciousness.

5.3 Epiphenomenalism and the will

Apart from these technical issues, we can ask whether the approaches that I have just outlined really get to grips with consciousness as I am defining it here. From the proposals described so far, it would seem that the role of consciousness might be any of the following: (1) to act as a random number generator so as to select one of the various possible outcomes embraced by a classical mixed state; (2) to implement the appropriate global action required by whatever interpretation we use (i.e. collapsing the wave function of the universe, splitting the universe, or entering an outcome in some sort of cosmic register of histories); (3) to take note mentally of what has been determined.

Looking at these possibilities critically, consciousness seems to be either magic, with a single thought having cosmic repercussions in splitting the universe; or patently inadequate, in leaving us with a mixed state but no single actual outcome; or both! There seems to be no role for the essence of consciousness, namely "what it is like": the accounts just described are strictly rational with no reference to the subjective.

I will shortly be describing more complex models which achieve more than those of London and von Neumann. But if we simply elaborate the mechanical processes of quantum theory so as to fix the technical problems, then we are left with a situation in which consciousness *does* nothing at all: it simply "lights up", as it were, the mechanical processes of the brain. In the terminology of consciousness studies, it is an *epiphenomenon* – i.e. a phenomenon that sits "on top of" the real business of the brain without actually doing anything. In so far as "I" am consciousness, it means that I am merely a passive onlooker in a mechanical though partly random world.

Epiphenomenalism cannot be dismissed as a possibility. Practising self-examination easily reveals that we are often unaware of the real motives for our decisions at the time when we execute them, giving support to Daniel Dennett's remark that, though we think that consciousness is the CEO of the mind, it is really the public relations office. In the light of the fundamental model of our two ways of knowing, however, we can easily discern the active role of consciousness. It lies not in the aspects of our thoughts that can be expressed as propositions—the aspect that Dennett (1991) takes for his concept of consciousness—but in the dynamics of our inner and outer relationships, the qualities and values that we bring to them and which arise from them. In addition, we might note that evolution does not, in our experience, produce complex appendages—such as epiphenomenal consciousness—without reason; so it is worth digging deeper.

As noted in §1.7,[p. 16] it appears to us from our experience that consciousness is not simply a passive recorder: as well as just soaking in the view, we are aware of a "will" which involves making decisions and turning these decisions into action. Henry Stapp, whose model of consciousness will be reviewed below, provides a succinct picture of the sort of will that might play an active role in shaping the world:

> What is not justified is the presumption... that *all* aspects of experience examined and reported are necessarily causal consequences solely of brain mechanisms. The structure of contemporary physics entails no such conclusion. This is particularly relevant to data from first-person reports about active, willfully directed attentional focus, and especially to data pertaining to which aspects of the stream of conscious awareness a subject chooses to focus on... Conscious effort itself can, justifiably within science, be taken to be a primary variable whose complete causal origins may be untraceable in principle, but whose causal efficacy in the physical world can be explained on the basis of the laws of physics. (Schwartz, Stapp and Beauregard, 2005, p. 1311)

Such attentional focus is indeed a positive action because it represents my choice to connect myself with one aspect of my surroundings rather than another. We may go further than this in expressing will through our desires to make the world conform, in large ways and in small, to our supposed needs. We have preconceptions about how the world should be and so we exert our will to the end that this expectation is realised, to create conformity between our desire and the perceived world. Sometimes, we must admit, this is achieved by our expectation causing us to see what we expect rather than what is actually there (Puri & Wojciulik, 2008). The question is, can it also affect the universe so that it becomes as I hope? On a mechanistic view of the universe the exercise of will in the sense of holding a desire for a particular pattern of the world has nothing to do with what the world is really like, and the only way to alter what is "out there" is to do it mechanically: willing is then no more than a brain state, which initiates appropriate muscular activity which then impacts on the world. The question that I want to explore, however, is: within our quantum world could our desires and expectations *in themselves* alter the world?

For example, if I have a passion to know whether the Higgs boson exists and what its mass is, then my will is going to be highly focussed on the outcome of an experiment that is being carried out to investigate this. Indeed, I may have a vested interest in some particular outcome being realised in order to vindicate my own theories and thereby win a Nobel Prize. If the outcome of a quantum observation really can be resolved through the observer's consciousness, and if consciousness is where the quantum buck stops in the von Neumann chain of events in a quantum experiment, then my will might play a major part in the resolution of a quantum superposition, and thereby influence the course of the universe. The mysteries of consciousness and of quantum theory are solved in one blow. This may seem to scientists patently ridiculous, though in many cultures it would be acceptable. But if conscious desires can play a part in collapsing the quantum state into a particular outcome, why could I not actually determine what the mass of the Higgs boson is through my own will? (I am ignoring here some issues of consistency.[66])

I shall explore this effect of a desire, attention, or preconception when considering the model of "assertion" below.p. 123 Before addressing this at the theoretical level, however, we should ask, is there any experimental evidence, one way or the other, as to whether this action of mind over matter actually happens? Can we, however strange it may seem, affect which way the quantum dice will fall by exerting our will? Confusingly, such evidence as there is does suggest that desire or intention can have an effect on scientific experiments, but only to the minutest extent. What we are looking for here, namely desire affecting material outcomes, is an example of "psychokinesis", a supposed or hypothetical possibility which has been extensively researched within parapsychology (Radin, 1997; Helfrich, 2007). An analysis combining a large number of experiments shows an effect that is *significant*, in the sense that it is very unlikely to have occurred by chance. However, the *effect size* (the ratio of the difference made by "willing" compared to the intrinsic variability of the effect) was extremely low, to such an extent that the effect could only be discerned by analysing the accumulated data from many experiments.

I consider this an important finding, both regarding the small effect size that tells us that consciousness cannot crudely "fix" the process of quantum collapse, and regarding the statistical significance of the effect, which indicates that consciousness does do something, but perhaps at a more subtle level than we are envisaging. The small effect size in psychokinesis experiments, however, has the side effect that it opens the way for sceptics to claim that the result could easily be obtained by fraud or by unconsciously motivated errors in experimental procedures (even though no critic has convincingly demonstrated where the defect actually lies). The judgment hinges on which seems subjectively more likely: that a group of perhaps well-meaning but fallibly human parapsychologists have been less than scrupulous in their experimental methods (though no such faults have been demonstrated in recent work), or that there are effects for which there is no known mechanism within physics as currently understood? I can sympathise with the more conventional physicists who would opt for the former. This underlines the need for a much clearer theoretical understanding of the relationship between consciousness and physics. We need to take the data seriously, while recognising the urgent need for a theoretical framework linking consciousness and quantum physics. Since consciousness is in its essence a relational phenomenon, while quantum physics is a matter of rational thought, this theoretical framework has to be a model[p. 82] of "what the propositional receives from the relational" (as in the "fourfold" of §3.3[p. 78]) regarding the relational process of consciousness.

5.4 Models of the action of consciousness

The extremes of the possible approaches to consciousness seem to be on the one hand a somewhat absurd magical view of a universe that is split into pieces by every thought, and on the other hand the uncomfortable alternative of epiphenomenalism together with a lack of any complete account of how mixed states can turn into definite outcomes. The next step is to review what credible models might be viable alternatives to epiphenomenalism that actually account for what happens.

The model that we are seeking needs to refine the local state of the seat of consciousness so as to represent a single outcome. This must be done in a way distinct from a simple measurement or observation, since that just takes us back into the measurement problem. In general it will not be linked to an external measurement (a special case), so that it will remain open to different "windows" of topos logic.[p. 96]

Before we start, it might be helpful here to give a simple image of the nature of consciousness as I have described it so far. (The diagram below should only be regarded as a rough hint.) Consciousness and brain are two aspects of the core being of an organism. I have given the label "being" to the sort of entity of which consciousness and brain are aspects, in the sense of a particular being — a characterisation that will be discussed in the next chapter. We might say that consciousness is to do with being as such, and in particular with being for itself, and "brain" is to do with form.[p. 24, e. 11] Consciousness understands existence through our relational subsystem, while the detailed nature of this being is understood by our propositional subsystem, as form.

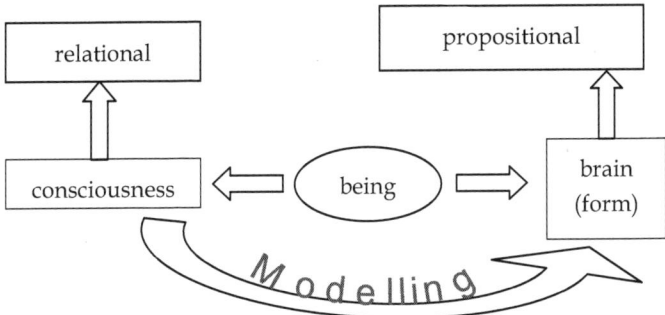

It is of the nature of the propositional and relational subsystems that the first analyses while the second synthesises. Consequently it is consciousness in itself that grasps the totality of being. Since brain (or at least a part or subsystem of brain identified as the seat of consciousness) and consciousness are aspects of one being, consciousness is grasping the whole nature of the brain as being, while the propositional is grasping the manifold complexity of the brain. In the diagram, "Modelling" is not a constituent of the brain in the way the others are (though it could be a constituent of my brain when I am thinking about this problem). It is what I propose that we should do order to understand how these components, with their disparate logics, might fit together. Issues around decoherence play a role in most of the models to be examined.

I will shortly look at three possible prototypes for a theory that might achieve this. They are Henry Stapp's use of the "Zeno effect" (which I have drawn on myself in Clarke, 2008), the "Orchestrated Objective Reduction" theory of Hameroff and Penrose, and my use there of "assertion" by consciousness rather than "observation", using an alternative version of the Zeno effect.

The Zeno effect

Conscious observation in quantum theory does two things: it puts the system being observed into a more definite state, and it brings to the observer the information about what that state now is. The Zeno effect as a process builds on this, so that the observer not only receives information, but can use this to manipulate the state in a desired manner. Specifically, it enables the consciousness of the observer, by continuously making rapidly repeated observations, to select a favourable quantum state, and then "lock" onto it, preventing it from drifting to another state as a result either of its internal mechanisms (the Hamiltonian) or external perturbations.

The reason why repeated observation locks the state is intuitively quite clear. If one observes a quantum system, then on the conventional approach it will collapse from a state that is open to any outcome to a state[p. 39] expressing a particular value for the quantity being observed. If the system is now left to itself, its state will then drift with time, as a result of its own internal dynamics and of its interaction with the environment, moving back into a superposition of (a) the state immediately after the observation with (b) a low amplitude different state corresponding to different values of the chosen quantity just measured. If, however, another measurement is made of this quantity before the state has drifted too far, then there is a high probability that the result will be the one obtained previously, and that the system will collapse back into the previous state.[67] (I am using the collapse interpretation here for simplicity, but it is easily reformulated in terms of histories.) So, by making rapidly repeated observations, the state can be "held" in the state into which it first collapses.

The effectiveness of this process depends on the ratio of two timescales: T_z, the "Zeno time" — the timescale on which the system drifts from one value to another; and T_m, the measurement time, specifying the minimum time between successive rapid measurements. The smaller the measurement time T_m compared to the Zeno time T_z, the longer the time for which the state is held. Eventually, because of the random nature of collapse, the state will "escape" into one with a different value, but the more rapidly one can make the measurements, the longer the state can be held in a definite value for the chosen observation.[68] This holding of the outcome by active conscious will is, for Stapp, the fundamental process whereby consciousness actually does something, rather than just receiving information.

There is no doubt about the existence of this effect in the laboratory, based on conventional measurement rather than consciousness (Itano *et al.*, 1990; Leibfried *et al.*, 2003, pp. 281ff). Moreover it is a candidate, at the molecular level, for the physical mechanism lying behind magnetic field detection in bird navigation (Kominis, 2009). In the next section we will examine how this can be put to use in understanding what consciousness can do.

5.5 Stapp's model

Henry Stapp developed his position in a series of papers from 1996, of which a collaborative work with Schwartz *et al.* (2005) is the most comprehensive. His approach to consciousness and quantum theory has many features in common with my own, but his key proposal is that the quantum Zeno effect can enable consciousness to manipulate the result of a quantum measurement.

We have noted in the table presented above that, in addition to the various interpretations of splitting, collapse, and so on, there are two rather different approaches to quantum measurement due to London and Bauer and due to von Neumann. Stapp's model mainly follows the latter, with the difference that he is concerned not so much with laboratory experiments but with human processes. I indicate this in the extension of the table given below, in which there is a further process added, termed by Stapp "process 3".

London & Bauer	Stapp	von Neumann	Proc.
Pure state	Mixed state		start
Recording	-	Recording	2
Collapse to outcome	Collapse to classical mixed state		1
-	Choice of Nature	-	3

Stapp follows von Neumann in regarding a "quantum state" from the start as being mixed, but not necessarily classical. Initially evolution takes place under the control of the Hamiltonian. "Collapse" ("process 1") then takes place as a result of consciousness—in the case of Stapp, specifically by the employment of the Zeno effect (Schwartz et al., 2005), resulting in a mixed statistical state: a classical statistical mixture of states corresponding to different outcomes. For the final step to a single outcome, Stapp quotes a rather vague description attributed to Dirac by Bohr (Bohr, 1958, p. 51; cf. Doyle, 2012) "that we [are] concerned with a choice on the part of 'nature'". Stapp (2007) assigns this step to a "von Neumann process 3".

Thus in Stapp's system consciousness chooses what observation to carry out on parts of the brain, and uses the Zeno effect in order to steer the nature of the observation in a particular direction. This choice, he stresses, is "described in mentalistic (i.e. psychological) language"

(Schwartz et al., 2005, p. 2), a concept essentially equivalent to my formulation of a "model" of the relational subsystem, except that I would argue that the model needs to deliver a non-standard logic rather than the standard logic of academic psychology. Once consciousness has determined the nature of this internal observation, there remains the problem of reaching one particular outcome for the observation.

One might object to Stapp's scenario on the grounds that, as in von Neumann's approach, the problem of a reduction to a mixed classical state is already achieved anyway by decoherence; so that consciousness is not actually adding anything unless it can produce a single outcome. This is true in the case of the observation of a physics experiment in which the outcome is being registered by a macroscopic "pointer" which the observer then notes. In the case, however, where consciousness is observing the small-scale structure of the brain itself—where there may be no clear "pointer basis" to define a particular window or observation—the Zeno effect could be used to narrow down this part of a selection.[69]

Moving on from this, we can now see that other possibilities are opened up. If the Zeno effect is being brought into play, it would seem that its role needs to be not that of creating a classical statistical state, but in steering this state to one particular outcome—thus avoiding the confusion between a mixture due to lack of data and a mixture inherent to the Hamiltonian evolution. Thus the general problem for our consciousness in implementing a Zeno effect is, how can it "grab" one particular quantum state and hang onto it long enough for it to become a stable part of a new reality?

There is an important distinction to be made here between the situation in the case of a physics experiment where the "system" is an artefact specially designed to amplify one property of the system rather than others, and the continuous dynamic of the human brain. In the latter case there is no neat distinction between the first experimental phase which determines the nature of the particular observation that is to be applied, and the conscious phase of extracting one particular value. If the "system" in question is a biological one such as a human brain, then the gap to be filled involves both the selection of the observation and the determination of the result. With this understanding, Stapp's model is a consistent process whereby consciousness resolves the ambiguities of quantum theory; but it still leaves unclear our understanding of how consciousness is actually doing it.

A significant factor in assessing this theory arises from the fact that, in any situation in which the Zeno effect operates, it is theoretically possible not merely to "hold" a result that has previously emerged purely randomly, but also to force the occurrence of a *desired* outcome. This goes beyond Stapp's basic model in which the final outcome arises purely randomly. Since, however, the possibility of determining the outcome of a future observation in advance would be very useful if we could do it, the question arises, why has evolution not produced this better model?

Only a small modification is required for us to be able to carry out this improved version of the Zeno effect. First, one makes occasional observations at intervals corresponding to the Zeno time T_z until the result is, by chance, the desired value. Then, having got this result, one switches to rapid measurements as described above in order to hold it in position. The overall length of time for which the desired outcome is present depends on the size of the minimum time between rapid measurements compared to the Zeno time. The smaller this measurement time, the greater the average time in which the *desired* result is present. The aim of consciousness would be to hold onto this result for long enough to enable it to be integrated into the large-scale structures of the brain. But is there in fact any evidence that this stronger version has in fact evolved, so that we can affect external events in this way? I will examine that question further below.

Size and the Zeno effect

We have already noted the importance of the physical size of the seat of consciousness, which affects both the extent of disturbance by the environment (decoherence) and the scope for the Zeno effect. Stapp argues that the action of consciousness is specifically on the synapses through which one neuron passes a signal to another (and in particular on the "calcium channels" of such synapses) since these are physically small enough to take part in a quantum event.

The size of the system involved, discussed above, is also important if the Zeno process is to be used, because the feasibility of the process depends on the values of the two timescales T_z and T_m discussed above.[p. 115] These change with the physical size of the system involved. The Zeno time T_z *decreases* as the energy of the system and the energy of the disturbances from the environment increase, an increase which occurs roughly as the cube of the size. On the other hand, the minimum size for T_m (the "measurement time", i.e. the shortest time in which a measurement can be done) can hardly[70] be smaller than the time taken for light to cross the system (the shortest possible communication time). This is also the time involved for the hyperbolic domains[e, 35] over which the state is averaged in generalised quantum theory.[71] This time clearly *increases* with the size of the system. The timescale for which the state can be held unchanged by the Zeno effect is given by the ratio T_z^2/T_m, and so as one considers successively larger systems there is a point where the light-crossing time is the same order as the Zeno time, after which the Zeno effect cannot take place. Very roughly (give or take a factor of 50 or so either way) the critical size is about the diameter of the nucleus of a biological cell. This rough argument certainly does not rule out a synapse as a point of operation of the effect. Importantly, a long, thin system will have a much larger Zeno time but a similar measurement time than fully 3D systems of the same size. This makes it likely that microtubules with be susceptible to the Zeno effect, and this could even extend to neural dendrites.[72]

The problem, however, is that the initial state of consciousness will be integrating a wide range of sensations, thoughts, and memories, and so needs to be associated with a large portion of the brain in order to access these thoughts. Then, on Stapp's account, it needs to perform a choice of measurement on the quantum states of one or many synapses, in such a way that the resulting state finally can link back effectively into a large portion of the brain in order to implement the choice that has been made. As is recognised, in a similar context, in the next model (that of Hameroff and Penrose), there is a need somehow to "orchestrate" the responses of many synapses if the consciousness of the human as a whole is to interact quantum mechanically with the rest of the world.

The seat and the brain

There is a further problem with the claim that consciousness carries out a Zeno process in order to achieve conscious wishes, concerned with how this mechanism fits into the bigger picture. Human consciousness is by its nature integrative: it is concerned with relationships and connections, not only with other beings but within itself. The awareness within consciousness of "what it is like to be me" correlates, presumably, with the overall large-scale systems of the brain rather than with the minutiae of the synapses in one particular neuron. Thus, if the start of consciousness lies in single neurons (or, as with Penrose and Hameroff's approach below, in even smaller organelles within cells), then these elements of consciousness need to be integrated (or, as with Penrose, "orchestrated") into the larger consciousness associated with "me". In other words, our consciousness needs to be hierarchical, as discussed above[p. 16] in connection with the "compound I". In the next chapter I will be discussing how this might take place.

The essence of consciousness, I have argued, is that it is to be understood via our relational subsystem. In its nature it is not a mechanical process that can be rationally mapped out: it is a freely flowing network of felt relationships that obey a different logic from the rational. It is an awareness whose scope seems unbounded, accessed more truly through meditation than through discursive thought. We need to put these qualities at centre stage if we are to understand consciousness. Only after that can we consider, with our propositional faculties, how we can best model what is going on in the rich landscape of the relational mind. I will be raising pointers towards this in the final chapter.

5.6 Orchestrated Objective Reduction

Stuart Hameroff and Roger Penrose (Hameroff, 1996; see also Hameroff, 1998) use a quite different mechanism in a different biological and theoretical context. So far in this chapter we have used the idea that, if consciousness has a quantum mechanical influence on the brain, then it probably has to act via one or more elements in the brain (parts of a cell such as organelles or synapses) that are small enough not to be so influenced by decoherence that their response would be essentially classical. In general the actual size varies strongly with the details of the biology involved, though very rough estimates can still be made. Recall, however, the discussion in §2.9[p. 58] which noted that when there is a large enough difference between the distribution of the masses of two superposed systems, then the geometry of their corresponding space-times is different by an amount that may be significant on the quantum level. At this point—where the system involved is heavier than a threshold mass (the "Planck mass")[73] of around 2×10^{-8} kg, corresponding to a size of the order of the body of a nerve cell—it no longer makes sense to use a conventional form of quantum theory that depicts quantum states as related to a *fixed* background space-time. This provides a natural threshold beyond which, according to Penrose, quantum phenomena have to "collapse" into classical ones.

Note that the physics here is fundamentally different from that assumed by Stapp, who sticks to conventional physics but has consciousness intervening via an observation. Penrose argues that conventional physics has to break down at this threshold mass for superposed systems: something has to give, whether consciousness is involved or not. Penrose then associates this collapse process with consciousness, and cites the defining characteristic of consciousness (on his view) as a breaking through from the mechanical processes of causality in the pre-conscious world into the imaginative and non-mechanical processes of consciousness. In his terminology, mechanical pre-conscious processes are "algorithmic" (i.e. obeying rules that could be implemented on a computer program), while the processes of consciousness can be "non-algorithmic".

Penrose's collaborator, Stuart Hameroff, is an Emeritus professor for Anesthesiology and Psychology, and so is familiar with the processes where anaesthetics act on brain cells so as to suppress consciousness. These suggest that changes in consciousness can indeed be brought about at the cellular level, and hence through Penrose's collapse process. The picture was then completed when they realised that organelles in the cell called microtubules might support processes reminiscent of those used in "quantum computing". (Microtubules are essential components of cells, providing mechanical traction for performing cell division and maintaining their internal shape. Their structure of regularly repeating units could, however, also act as conduits for processing information.)

One problem with this idea was that a single microtubule was far lighter than the Planck mass (and the movements of its individual units would be even less effective). Therefore the changes in microtubules would have to be "orchestrated" throughout the cell in order to activate Penrose's postulated role of consciousness in quantum collapse. This tension between the scale on which quantum effects seem to happen and the presumed scale of the seat of our consciousness runs through these models. It is made explicit by Penrose and Hameroff, though it is not clear just how this "orchestration" will work. In view of this, an essential part of building models has to be a study of the hierarchical nature of seats of consciousness: the way in which an extensive seat can accommodate within it many smaller, perhaps microscopic, seats which are both carriers of consciousness in their own right and also contributors to the larger consciousness. We have noted this earlier (§1.6 p. 16) and it will form a part of the role of cosmic consciousness in our examination of "the choice of nature" below.p. 126

5.7 Assertion

For an alternative model that can translate consciousness into propositional terms, I want to introduce the notion of *assertion* as an alternative to observation. The motive for this particular concept lies in the idea that the logic that models the relational mind handles negation differently from that of the propositional mind. In the propositional:

1) to every proposition there is another associated proposition that is its negation;
2) the negation of a negation restores the original proposition; and,
3) given a context and a proposition that is defined on the whole of this context, for any instance within this context the proposition is either true or false.

We have already noted that (1) is denied by Matte Blanco ("there is no negation"[e. 52]). (2) and (3) are essentially equivalent and false for the quantum logic introduced in chapter 4, which in part follows "intuitionist" logic in which there are propositions that are neither true nor false.[74]

In quantum physics it is often convenient to handle negation by reducing a physical observation to the testing of a succession of (compatible) yes-no questions. E.g. "is the particle in the left half of this chamber?"; "is the particle in the left half of the region defined by the previous test?"; "is the magnetisation of the particle upwards?" In the context defined by these particular tests, if the answer to any one is "yes" then the answer to its alternative proposition (e.g. "is the particle in the right half on the chamber") is "no". Thus an experiment for testing this proposition is in fact an experiment that tests for the pair of alternatives "left or right" and whose outcome is either one or the other. In the wider context where quantum logic comes into play, however, truth—as noted in chapter 4—becomes many-valued and obeys intuitionistic rules. Thus when it comes to modelling the role of consciousness, which is very different from the role of an experiment that is set up to investigate a strictly propositional question, we should not assume that an attempted observation of a happening A is at the same time an observation of a happening *not-A*: we should allow "one-sided" observations that do not have a corresponding negation. This might be particularly the case, for instance, if I was particularly interested in A but indifferent to *not-A*. In that case, rather than "is it A or *not-A*" it is a matter of "let it be A!" I will call the act of this sort of one-sided observation an *assertion* of A.

In a standard physics experiment there are always strict yes-no divisions (and a quantitative measurement, e.g. "how massive is it?", can be reduced to a succession of such divisions). A yes-no experiment establishes a mixed local state that already builds in a symmetrical dichotomy between A and *not-A* before this state is communicated to the brain. By contrast, an *assertion* that arises in consciousness is non-symmetrical and could plausibly have a different effect on the state of the brain than that which is produced in the case of physical experiment.

We are here in the realm of investigating what might be possible, with very limited evidence; so we are looking for likely hypotheses. In this spirit I will proceed with what seems a reasonable possibility: namely, that after an assertion of A either nothing happens, with the occurrence of A not confirmed and no change taking place in the quantum state; or that A is observed, and the state collapses (or the equivalent in other interpretations) into one in which the consequences of A enter into the brain. For a formulation of this in terms of mixed states, see the endnote[75].

It is worth noting that assertion can be applied as a repeated operation so as to force a particular outcome. Moreover, the Zeno effect can be modified so that it selects a particular outcome (rather than just restricting the scope to a mixture of outcomes as in Stapp's usage). In these cases, assertion is much more effective. Thus assertion can be viewed as a version of the Zeno effect, and hence as a variation on Stapp's approach.

Once we bring assertion into the discussion, the prospects for experimental investigation become much brighter than was the case with the psychokinesis experiments discussed above. If consciousness really can interact with the brain in a way that is effectively modelled by assertion, then a much wider range of parapsychology experiments, many with reasonable effect sizes as well as high significance, can be related to a scientific model (Clarke, 2008). Although there is a long way to go before the tentative models discussed here can be seriously tested through parapsychology (and even further in testing through physics), this seems at present the best chance of both understanding quantum theory and providing an adequate theoretical underpinning for parapsychology. Without such an underpinning, parapsychology is destined to remain at best a semi-science, and for many a pseudo-science.

5.8 The choice of nature

The models of consciousness so far described are based on two ideas: that there is a clear division between the classical and the quantum, and that consciousness is strictly involved with the latter. If we consider again, however, the table of Stapp's model above,[p. 116] then a new possibility arises. The problem with his formulation is that consciousness is brought in at the point where the state is transformed to a "classical mixed state". But since that stage in the sequence is already taken care of by decoherence, the place where consciousness is needed is at the next stage where Stapp resorts to "choice of nature". At first it might seem that this is impossible, because once we have a "classical" state, then we assume that Newtonian physics rules and consciousness has no place; but, strictly speaking, the action of decoherence does not change the physics from quantum into Newtonian. It merely changes the quantum state into a local quantum state[e. 16] whose behaviour is, in most cases, indistinguishable from a state in classical physics.

Suppose that we adopt a model in which consciousness is applied at this last stage to choose a particular outcome, while we recognise that the "states" we are talking about are quantum states (either pure or mixed), not classical states. It will mean that consciousness probably cannot play so many quantum tricks, such as "assertion", in order to twist the universe to its will, although this might be possible using very small seats of consciousness.

We already know from psychokinesis experiments, however, that this sort of thing is at best very weak: it is clearly not the case that consciousness can simply come in at the last stage and fix its favourite outcome. Instead, we need to consider the wider picture, by considering the global context of a particular being. The local state is a reduction of the quantum state of the cosmos, and consciousness at a particular moment in a particular being acts by determining a particular window and registering this in a generalised history. As Wheeler claimed, the real choice—the Choice of Nature—takes place at this cosmic level, where the whole network of observations are taken into account together. At this level the global statistics associated with generalised histories take on a decisive role. Our own decisions and desires are set out not in isolation but within the context of cosmic consciousness.

5.9 What does consciousness do to consciousness?

So far in this chapter we have (implicitly) considered only the effect of consciousness on the quantum mechanical aspects of the mind, with the problem of finding a more complete model of quantum theory at the forefront. "Consciousness", however, denotes a whole universe of being that is only truly accessible through relational knowing; and it is perhaps this aspect that is most important for humanity. We have, for example, cited Eckhart's experience[e. 8] of *working* at the most profound, universal, relational level—a level referred to by Eckhart, for his acknowledged want of a better word, as "God". We might also, with some straining of language, think of this as what consciousness does to/with consciousness. If I were to consider this in depth it would take us far afield; but some consideration is vital to any understanding of consciousness.

I have iterated the point that consciousness is in itself simple, and so we might expect this realm of doing to be itself simple—which, as Eckhart, Heidegger, and many others exemplify, does not mean that it will be accessible or comprehensible! Perhaps the most direct clue to what consciousness does from the viewpoint of the relational (in the sense of actual being) derives from Spinoza's concept of *conatus* (Spinoza, 1677).[76] He writes:

> Everything, in so far as it is in itself ("in se est"), endeavours ("conatur") to persist in its own being... The endeavour ("conatus"), wherewith everything endeavours to persist in its own being, is nothing else but the actual essence of the thing in question. (See also Mathews, 2003, p. 48)

So every actual being, whatever else that it might do, "endeavours to persist in its own being". And this action is not an optional add-on to a being: it is the essence of its being. This concept is powerfully unifying and "simple" (in the sense noted above). It clarifies what a being is (a point we come to in the next chapter) as well as specifying the core of what it does. The essence of the seat of consciousness is its property of being conscious, and hence the essence of what it does is to maintain its consciousness: an essentially conscious being is a thing that maintains its consciousness.

In a sense Spinoza is simply putting into a metaphysical form what we tend to take for granted from a more mechanistic perspective: that life is by definition dynamic and enduring, so that anything that is either fleeting or inert cannot be regarded as living.

What this concept means in practice will depend on the context. In the case of humanity, our consciousness revolves around our relationship with the world, and so what this consciousness does, at its heart, is the nurturing of this relationship—even when it might seem from the propositional perspective that it is destroying that relationship. This action will involve maintaining itself in a state which reflects the aspects of the world that impinge on it. If a microtubule is conscious, then its essence might be the execution of very basic chunks of quantum-logic computation (here I resort to propositional language, because there is no way whatever in which I can know what it is like to be a microtubule!) and what it does at its core is to maintain this computational capacity.

The effect of the *conatus* of consciousness, while related to the properties of life, is *categorically* different from the effects of evolution and learning on life. The latter is linked to memory, in a generalised sense that includes the storage of information in genes and the storage of memory in the body — particularly in the brain for animals. *Conatus*, manifesting from essential being, is not bound to time in this way. Its model in the propositional is Hartle's approach to quantum physics in which it is the totality of events in space-time that determines the probability of a history. In our "normal" state of consciousness we have little access to this: the nearest we get is to conceive of the action of consciousness as taking place *now* (a concept that, according to Boethius, is a shadow of the eternal Now of mystical awareness). So we can conceive of *conatus* asserting the being of consciousness in each moment.

This conception of consciousness now sheds light on its potentially hierarchical aspects. To return to the Penrose-Hameroff model of consciousness discussed in section 5.6, if the consciousness of the microtubules in a cell are "orchestrated" in their activity throughout the cell as a whole, then we can expect the cell itself to be conscious as a result.

Synopsis

- Consciousness terminates the chains of increasingly broad quantum events and selects "my world" out of a quantum soup of possibility.
- The work of Stapp provides a good framework for this, but it stands in need of a clear process that produces a specific outcome at the end of quantum events.
- The Zeno effect can be generalised so as to provide a stronger mechanism whereby consciousness can have material consequences.

- Parapsychology already provides informative evidence for the very low effect size of any direct psychokinetic action of consciousness, but this discipline stands in need of an underpinning by physics.
- The gap between the characteristic length-scales accessible by quantum phenomena and the possible length-scale of the seat of human consciousness remains a problem. A hierarchical structure within conscious beings could solve this and give content to Penrose's idea of "orchestration".
- Spinoza's "*conatus*", as interpreted by Mathews, is proposed as a model of what consciousness "does to consciousness".
- The final emergence of a particular outcome for a quantum observation is determined by cosmic consciousness.

Six

What Things Are Conscious?

So far "consciousness" has implicitly meant human consciousness, because this is the only sort that we know directly. Most would agree, however, that at least mammals are conscious. Whether or not a being is conscious depends not on its whole anatomy, but on the part — termed the "seat of consciousness" in §1.6[p. 14] *— which implements its consciousness. Because consciousness is a fundamental phenomenon independent of the complexity or otherwise of what a being may be conscious of, one cannot place a lower limit of complexity on what a seat of consciousness might be. This leads to panpsychism: that everything is conscious. And "everything" leads to "what is a thing?" I cannot answer this, but can give suggestions as to how an answer might be found with the aid of quantum theory.*

6.1 Chasing consciousness

I will begin from a relational point of view. From this aspect I see consciousness as something that I instantly recognise in another being, as a result of entering, perhaps fleetingly and barely recognised, into a relationship with that being. It is not something that I work out logically. Consciousness might be hard to define, but essentially, in myself or in another, it is simple. The appearance of complexity arises not from consciousness itself, but from the complexity of signals entering, or generated by, the seat of consciousness.

Meister Eckhart described seeing a tiny beetle and, recognising that it is conscious, he identifies it with the source of all consciousness, declaring that "*there* is God". This recognition is something *seen*, but seen with "the eye of contemplation".[77] What Eckhart recognises in the creature is *istigkeit* (isness) and for him "isness is God".

We today would call isness "being"; so let us call those things that have consciousness "beings" (though this is admittedly awkward, grammatically).[78] When I recognise a being, it is in front of me as a whole;[79] its isness is in every part of it and to separate its parts would be to annihilate its being. This wholeness is the nature of what we are ultimately looking for.

At the end of chapter 1 I noted the strong evidence that once we take into account the data of our own relational knowing as well as that from our propositional knowing then it makes sense to define consciousness as a purely subjective "what it is like to be" which is not confined to human beings. Consciousness in this sense

- is best grasped by our relational, rather than by our propositional way of knowing (§3.1[p. 67]),
- is distinct from self-consciousness in the sense of reflexive consciousness (§1.5 [p. 12]),
- is distinct from information processing (since there is no reason to suppose that mechanical information processing is accompanied by consciousness),
- is a candidate for resolving the problem of how structure appears in the universe (§2.10[p. 62]),
- is essentially simple (§1.8[p. 20]).

From a propositional perspective these bullet points, while they define what we are talking about, are not very constructive in telling us what consciousness really *is*. Some are negative: they tell us what consciousness is *not*, and what it is *not* restricted to; but we still need to know what it is and where it is to be found. In this chapter we are trying to grasp the second of these problems, that of locating which systems are conscious. In other words, and roughly speaking, where do we find consciousness? We have already noted in section 1.6[p. 15] that it is unhelpful to ask where consciousness is in itself, but useful to ask for the whereabouts of the "seat" of the consciousness of a particular being: the physical correlate of consciousness. The place of a seat of consciousness is more localised than the place of a being (as defined above). In the case of a human, the being is the whole person because it is this whole that we encounter in relationship; but the seat of consciousness might, for instance, be some small part of the brain.

As well as being more localised, the place of the seat of consciousness is a more complex notion than that of a being because of a confusing factor, namely that consciousness can be hierarchical with nested seats one inside another (as noted earlier: §1.6[p. 16]). Here we are concerned with nesting in which the smaller part contributes from its consciousness into the larger, rather than cases where one seat of consciousness in physically contained within another completely distinct seat, with the inclusion being incidental, neither consciousness taking any notice of the other.[80]

Within this concept of nesting are models of the mind like Freud's notion of the unconscious, models that posit a number of interacting areas of different modes of consciousness, of which one is identified with the "I" ("ego") but all participate in what constitutes the human mind. This points to a possible variety of seats of human consciousness within ourselves (or within our brains) which contribute to an overall consciousness. Indeed, as Lockwood (1989) has convincingly argued, as we introspect our own processes we can see a penumbra of conscious processes which we can choose to include or exclude within our verbally-linked train of thought. In this case one can imagine a genuinely hierarchical process in which lower levels actually contribute to the higher levels rather than simply being in the same place as those. In this case there can be a functional hierarchy without their necessarily being a physical hierarchy: if, as seems likely, human consciousness arises from processes that are distributed over different regions of the brain, rather than from a single Cartesian "organ of consciousness", then there is a plausible possibility of multiple overlapping seats of subsidiary consciousnesses.

The clearest example of this from the previous chapter is in Penrose and Hameroff's "Orchestrated Objective Reduction" where the most likely possibility is that a cell is conscious through the hierarchy of its conscious microtubules. In all the examples there, one would expect that a distributed sub-network covering much of the brain would also be conscious through a hierarchy of its neurons — but we know too little of the brain, or of consciousness, to be more specific.

Continuing the quest for seats of consciousness, recall that in chapter 1 I eliminated any sort of criterion for consciousness based on information processing, because, as Velmans (2000) puts it, one can imagine any information processing happening "in the dark" just as easily as imagining its being conscious. Criteria for consciousness such as "sensation" are unhelpful, because sensation is just information processing that happens to be conscious, which makes the criterion circular. We need a more radical approach than these. What suggests itself is *panpsychism*: the proposition that everything is conscious — an idea with a long and respectable pedigree (de Quincey, 2002; Skrbina, 2005; Mathews, 2003). I shall approach this first from a propositional perspective, and then from a relational one.

6.2 A propositional view of panpsychism

At first panpsychism sounds like a neat (if somewhat bizarre) solution; but then a further problem presents itself. If every-thing is conscious, what counts as a "thing"?[e. 62] Is a "living room suite", consisting of a sofa and two chairs, a conscious "thing"? No, because this example clearly consists of three things, not one thing. So could each chair and sofa on its own be conscious? Well, no also, because these are really equally multiple, consisting of bits and pieces nailed and strung together; surely a "thing" that is conscious has to be homogeneously connected in some way? But then consider the science fiction novel *The Black Cloud* by Fred Hoyle, in which the earth was occupied (or rather, lorded over) by an alien creature made up of a large number of separate particles linked together only by exchanging radio signals. Hoyle created a plausible depiction of this "character" being a conscious thing, even though the solid particles of it were completely separate. Moreover, the electromagnetic impulses implementing the Black Cloud's organisation could not be separated from the electromagnetic field that permeates the entire universe. If this is a candidate for a "thing" or being, couldn't one designate any arbitrary region of the universe as a being? Moreover, if we were to take this *laissez-faire* attitude, on which *anything* has the necessary "unity", I could subdivide it to produce more arbitrarily small conscious beings.

If panpsychism is to make sense, it requires a criterion that singles out those things that are seats of consciousness, rejecting arbitrary "stuff" like chairs but not being so restrictive as to exclude non-human animals, for instance, that we would want to include.

6.3 Things

So what might this criterion be? It is hard to answer this, but drawing from the lines of argument so far, I will propose three main ideas that could lead to a defining criterion for the sort of thing that is conscious; that is, for a "being" in the sense of §6.1.

In the previous section we have ruled out a living room suite as a being, because it was merely a collection.

Whitehead (1978 [1929]) called such collections "aggregates", as distinct from "actual entities" which have an internal unity. Fred Hoyle's "Black Cloud", on the other hand, could be a candidate for a "being" because the electromagnetic field that permeates it does constitute some sort of unity. In order to rule out living room suites we require a criterion that reflects unity, but in order to include the Black Cloud[81] it must not depend on the contiguity of the parts of the thing. So the first idea is:

▶ Unity. An arbitrary collection does not count as a "being", because it has no inherent unity.

Next, we have noted that performing information processing is not relevant here because this refers to what is the input to consciousness, which could equally well take place without being conscious; and by the same token neither is any criterion based on what a thing *does* in the sense of mechanical[82] action. We need something that goes beyond these mechanical criteria. Since Newtonian theory is of its nature mechanical, it seems promising to look for a quantum theoretical criterion. This is, of course, also supported by the arguments for a role for consciousness in quantum theory that we have explored in the preceding chapters, and particularly the suggestion of London and Bauer (chapter 2 and above[p. 116]) that consciousness acts effectively as part of the process of quantum measurement. More generally, consciousness could have a role in resolving quantum mixtures (§2.5[p. 39]) into distinct states. The idea that consciousness is essential for drawing out a definite result for an observation is for me convincing: there seems to be no viable alternative at present. If this is so, it means that there is a connection between quantum phenomena and consciousness. Our second idea is thus:

▶ Quantum properties. A conscious being is likely to be constituted in a way that naturally engages with quantum processes.

This formulation is deliberately very vague, and carries the danger of including almost everything. If we consider matter at the quantum level, then any region, however large or small, will trivially satisfy this. The idea needs to be refined. Part of a "being", such as half of a seat of consciousness, is likely to be non-functional as far as consciousness is concerned; or, if it is conscious it will constitute a different "being" from the whole, suggesting the following idea.

▶ Completeness. A being must be complete—which could be defined as being a structure that cannot be enlarged unless the additions are superfluous or the structure becomes essentially different. It is maximal with respect to its own characteristic operations.

One natural way of satisfying these requirements might be to draw on the notion of entanglement, using the idea that entanglement brings separated regions into a sort of unity. So a possible idea for pinning down the seats of consciousness is to require, as their defining property, that their parts are connected through a large amount of quantum entanglement so as to establish a wholeness. Then the extent of the seat could be defined as the boundary beyond which this entanglement faded.

I explored this in Clarke (2007), defining a seat of consciousness as "a maximal region of space that is internally connected by a high degree of quantum entanglement". A convenient measure of quantum entanglement between two different regions of space is the extent to which two propositions,[p. 93] one defined in each of the two regions, can be correlated—a measure based on the statistical property of "covariance" between such propositions. If the quantum states in the two regions are not entangled at all this measure is zero, rising to 1 for maximum entanglement. The idea was that the more strongly[83] different parts of a being are entangled, the more there are correlations between the way they behave. Entanglement would thus confer a dynamic wholeness on the region being considered. Since this criterion uses only fundamental quantum properties, with no reference to particular structures, it implies that seats of consciousness are ubiquitous—as is required for the approach of panpsychism that I am proposing.

This approach works well for small regions in which a well-defined local state can be established by the processes described in the previous chapter. Specific entanglements can be defined, with significance at the implicational level. In addition, for small regions models such as "assertion" can maintain these entanglements and thereby implement the implicational concept of "*conatus*" described above.[p. 128]

This links in with the idea of "decoherence" (§2.7[p. 44]). Within a closely knit collection of particles (e.g. an atom) each particle is closely entangled with the others so as to produce, in the sense we are exploring now, a highly integrated system. But as we consider systems occupying larger regions of space, the interaction of particles with the environment as a whole rises, and soon is comparable or greater than its interaction with other parts of the system, which is the essence of decoherence.

As a result, when explored in more detail[84] it turns out that this argument alone implies that it is impossible for an object the size of the human brain, say—or even a small anatomical part of the brain—to exhibit quantum effects, because any quantum state that might emerge seems to be immediately swallowed up in the entanglements of the brain with the distant environment. For this reason Hameroff and Penrose (1996) restricted consciousness to microtubules and Stapp restricted the quantum action to neural synapses, as described in the previous chapter. Similarly there does not at present seem to be any mechanism that can implement the hierarchical building of larger units of consciousness from small ones. A broader canvas seems to be needed, that takes the relational more into consideration.

Since figures for the size of a seat of consciousness remain stubbornly and radically too small, the relational now enters as the essential element: but that does not mean that the propositional is to be jettisoned. As McGilchrist argued, the modern human predicament comes not just from a neglect of the relational, but also (and I would say, even more so) from our inability to maintain a natural flow between the two.

6.4 The cosmos

The problem of decoherence is grounded in the conventional way of thinking about quantum states within the brain (or within any seat of consciousness). It is drawn from the viewpoint of an external observer looking down onto the smaller elements of systems, with no detailed knowledge of the larger picture. The advent of quantum cosmology, however, provides another imaginary perspective, though not one which we can actually occupy: the perspective of the Hatter in the treacle well parable of §2.10 .p. 58 As he thinks about quantum cosmology he imagines that he is "looking" at the pure quantum state that is the quantum universe as a whole. Nagel (1986) has referred to this, pejoratively, as the "God's eye view" and has cogently argued that it is spurious, because it is a "view from nowhere" which it is impossible to occupy.

Against Nagel, however, is the fact that almost all physics is motivated by a sort of thinking that pretends to come from a God-like hypothetical viewpoint that is unreachable in practice—in most cases for fundamental reasons rather than practical ones. We can think of Einstein when he was young trying to imagine what light would look like if you were travelling at its speed, of the intense evening arguments between Bohr and Einstein at the Solvay conference based on Gedankenexperimente (thought-experiments) which, though impossible to perform, revealed flaws in the other's argument. The "view from nowhere" of Quantum Cosmology, of the quantum cosmos as a whole, is a thriving part of physics, and "the entire quantum universe" is as common a concept as the many other abstract and invisible entities that are commonplace in physics. It is now an integral part of modern thinking.

The importance of the view of quantum cosmology to this book is that it seems to offer a way round decoherence. On a "selection" view of generalised quantum theory,[e. 40] the universe does not collapse, there is no need to "trace out" the part of the universe that is hidden from the experimenter, and the state of the universe is always a pure state. Thus for the cosmos there is no decoherence and the way is open for consciousness to manipulate experience, selecting judicious propositions to enter into the generalised histories of beings.

From this imaginary vantage point, the cosmos itself is a being. It is in a pure quantum state and there is nothing outside it to adulterate this state. Since its parts have been constantly interacting with each other it possesses a high degree of internal entanglement, suggestive of unity. Therefore, it is a being. From this viewpoint other beings inside it are components of the quantum state, which preserve their own purity, and decoherence is an illusion projected on these components by internal observers who cannot see the whole picture.

The cosmos is the top level in the hierarchy of nested beings which we have already noted in §6.1.[p. 133] In the previous sections we have struggled with the problem of how to piece together tiny beings into ones whose consciousness is increasingly complex; with a cosmic perspective we switch to the problem of how the cosmos separates itself into beings of progressively decreasing size. In other words, we need to understand the relationship between cosmic consciousness, if there is such a thing, and individual consciousnesses.

The new quantum logic has a crucial role here as it describes the variety of "windows" — incompatible on Aristotelian logic but a fertile bank of new contexts within our new logic. It may seem that this picture is heading towards the idea of a "splitting/branching universe" that was described earlier; but our new understanding of logic and psychology gives a very different story. The new quantum logic presents us with an interface between the propositional and the relational mind. Because the process is steered by consciousness, consciousness can lead our thought from the propositional of the mathematics of quantum theory to the relational of its interpretation, as beings emerge from the ultimate simplicity of the first emergence of the cosmos.

From this viewpoint cosmos thus has some analogies to Divinity, in a form not unlike that proposed by Whitehead (1978)[85] and other process philosophers. So "being" becomes "Being" with a capital letter, and starts to take on a more tendentious aspect. From our previous viewpoint the primary problem was how to maintain the *internal wholeness* and integrity of beings as one progressed to larger structures, considering conventional quantum theory and hence the propositional mind; now we are concerned with the *separation* of beings through the division of larger ones, in which the connection with Whitehead's "God" suggests that we need to use the relational mind.

Thinking in this mode takes me into considering traditional approaches to Being, particularly those from the Abrahamic traditions. The obvious difference is between the religious tendency in these traditions to personalise God and the scientific tendency — one might say "imperative" — to depersonalise the absolute. This leads many authors to make a sharp dichotomy between the (physical) cosmos and "God" as an absolute. Teilhard de Chardin was less extreme, but he notes that "...modern man is obsessed by the need to depersonalize (or impersonalize) all that he most admires... [one reason] is the discovery of the sidereal world—which is such a vast subject that it seems to destroy all proportion between our own existence and the dimensions of the cosmos around us."[86] Many students of cosmology like myself would hardly sympathise with this negative reaction to the cosmos, reminiscent of Pascal's "The eternal silence of these infinite spaces terrifies me".[87] For us, the universe is charged with an amazing beauty. If we were to regard the cosmos as itself a seat of consciousness, then this would, in Christian terms, be moving more towards concepts like McFague's (2006) view of the universe as "The body of God". We would be making universal Teilhard's merely planetary concept of the "noosphere". I think of this concept as being more general than Teilhard's concept. He applied it to the community of humans on the earth, whereas I apply it to all conscious beings.

But let us, despite these often unhelpful views, turn to the Hebrew and Christian[88] traditions. We then find many instances where the act of making a division—the core aspect of the differentiation of the homogeneous Big Question Mark into individual beings—is regarded as a vital part of creation. It is present in Genesis 1:6, where God (Elohim) proclaims "Let there be a firmament in the midst of the waters, and let it divide the waters from the waters";[89] it recurs in the story of the parting of the water of the Red/Reed Sea through the mediation of Moses; and it is central in the ritual of the parting of the water of the font in the Christian vigil before Easter[90]—the most pivotal moment in the ecclesiastical year, originally the only rite at which new members could enter the Church through baptism in the waters, on a night where "heaven and earth are joined".

These examples take us to the heart of the relational mind, to the nature of relationship itself, about which more can now be said from this new context. The vital point arising from the examples just listed is that relationship is different from experience. Relationship is distinctively the domain of the relational mind. Experience, on the other hand, is the role of consciousness which enters into most of the 9 subsystems which Teasdale and Barnard (1993) describe in their model (stopping at 9 for convenience rather than completion).

The pre-eminent insight into this distinction between experience and relationship is given by Martin Buber (2004). He describes the former as a process whereby "Man travels over the surface of things and experiences them. He extracts knowledge about their constitution from them: he wins an experience from them. He experiences what belongs to the things" (p. 17).[91] Relationship, on the other hand, is a meeting of *beings*, not an extraction of information about what the observer superficially takes for "things". Experience belongs to "the primary word *I-It*".[e. 41] Relationship, on the other hand, belongs to the primary word *I-Thou*. It is an encounter with the full isness of the Other, who is "a *Thou* and fills the heavens".

This is closely related to the stance taken by Ferrer (2002, p. 23) who carefully demolishes "intrasubjective reductionism (i.e. the reduction of spiritual and transpersonal phenomena to individual inner experience)". Spiritual phenomena are fundamentally relational and so must be distinguished from experiences.

These scattered ideas suggest an alternative approach to the criteria for a being. Instead of starting with the medium-sized objects — microtubules, synapses, etc. — and then looking to quantum theory in order to build them into larger conscious systems, we could start with the cosmos and examine how it could develop diversity and multiplicity within itself, using for our thinking our relational faculties as much as our propositional.

Synopsis

- The question of "what things are conscious?", in the context of our definition of consciousness, amounts to "what is a being?" It is a fundamentally relational issue.
- Modelling this question for the propositional leads to requiring a very broad criterion for beings, in the spirit of panpsychism. The main points that it must cover are unity, the manifestation of quantum properties, and completeness.
- The main impediment to this is presence of decoherence which, when the topic is analysed "from the bottom up", prevents a seat of consciousness from becoming large enough to be compatible with our human experience. This problem is essentially that of providing a concrete account of Hameroff's "orchestration".
- The solution appears to involve a "top-down" approach starting with the pure state of cosmos itself (when viewed through the generalised histories approach). On this view the cosmos is a being.
- The design of the top-down approach requires the modelling of relational accounts of the process of division into subsystems.

Seven

A New Programme for Consciousness Research

Rather than focussing solely on a modelling approach within quantum theory, the solution to the problem of consciousness requires active work in integrating the propositional and the implicational. This requires drawing on a wider range of relational aspects, in particular by including spirituality. In this area modelling becomes replaced by praxis. Achieving this requires awareness of the particular sensitivities and pitfalls surrounding spirituality.

7.1 The central aim

Until recently the study of consciousness has been divided into two areas, with little inter-communication between them: on the one hand careful analytical academic discussion of consciousness as a human faculty (perhaps analogous to such faculties as digestion or respiration); and on the other hand spiritually inspired speculation about consciousness as a universal animating principle in the universe. One main aim of this book has been to bridge this gap by focussing on the basic problem underlying this and many other issues that encumber the study of consciousness, namely the *de facto* separation of our two principle cognitive subsystems, the relational and the propositional. Academic research has focussed on the propositional, to the neglect of the relational — in the case of physics, exclusively so. However, consciousness (as I define it here) is mainly understood through the relational subsystem. So to make further progress in consciousness studies we have to reconnect these two subsystems, so that both of them can contribute constructively to this field. And that means integrating the academic study of consciousness with our relational life-experience of consciousness.

From this perspective, the various approaches to consciousness exemplify abuses of both science and spirituality, driven by blockages to the understanding of each by those who study the other. In order to understand this, it will be helpful here to spell out more distinct aspects of these misunderstandings, including an examination as to how the propositional way of knowing makes sense of the relational way, and vice versa. We can thus draw on the earlier idea of a fourfold division in our thinking:[p. 78] to the propositional and the relational this adds what the propositional receives from the relational and what the relational receives from the propositional.

Overcoming these blocks and weaknesses cannot happen merely by juxtaposing the two ways of knowing in a suitably structured manner; firstly, because their essential qualitative difference militates against any simple form of juxtaposition; and secondly, because our relational knowing has always been regarded as the inferior, "Cinderella subject" in relation to our propositional knowing. This neglect of the relational seems to require specific rebalancing in order to rehabilitate relational knowing of consciousness into academic discourse.

Because of these factors, the terms of the discussion now change. There are sensitive issues that have to be handled with care: most notably, morality and religion. Moral issues arise when we consider our relationships — these are the stuff of the relational subsystem. We experience relationships with other humans, with members of other species (particularly companion animals), and in many cases with less defined entities such as groves, mountains, or ecosystems. Our concepts of these things are shaped by our relationships. We feel that they have value in themselves and therefore play a particular part in our own consciousness. Or we may feel that our relationship with them is a relationship with another conscious being, and that therefore any conception of consciousness must, if it is to be faithful to our experience, include these as conscious beings. To deny this becomes not merely a logical *non sequitur*, but an affront to our own being.

The case of religion is just as sensitive. By "religion" I mean not its propositional theories and teachings, but a relational context for our encounters with states that we regard as having a greater reality than "normal" life — a topic we touched on earlier.[p. 18] These encounters often lead us to place the source of our individual consciousness in the greater, comprehensive consciousness that is experienced in such encounters. Particular problems then arise when we try to make sense of what is experienced, bringing in propositional understanding. The notion of "God" is particularly problematic — it is frequently a hybrid construct that makes little sense from either a propositional or relational perspective.

We could opt out of the difficulties by keeping science and religion separate, as was attempted in approaches such as that of Stephen J. Gould's (2002 [1999]) "non-overlapping magisteria", a purely propositional attempt to accommodate religion and science. But this would be to give up the hope of moving forward to a more integrated pattern of knowing. Our future aim therefore needs to be directed to connecting, within individuals and societies, and with appropriate sensitivity, our propositional and relational knowing of consciousness. This is all very new territory, which I will, in the rest of this final chapter, illustrate through a few particular topics.

7.2 The pitfalls of the transliminal

The sensitivity of this area is exemplified by the phenomenon referred to in §2.4 p. 34 in which apparently well-informed writers describe a technical term, such as the quantum state, as if it were God, in such a way that they abuse both physics and spirituality. In many cases (e.g. Laszlo, 2004; cf. Clarke & King, 2006) this amounts to a reinvention of physics, setting out a picture of quantum theory which would more comfortably fit their own conceptions of a spiritual universe. This activity ranges from romantic extensions and decorations of physics (Zohar, 1990) to the complete construction of physics from scratch, often within mini-communities (Laszlo, 2004).

Rationally speaking it is not hard to see what is going on here. We live in a culture in which a gap has opened up between our relational knowing and our propositional knowing, and these writers are addressing topics which necessarily have a foot in both camps, as I have here. Because of the gap between the two ways of knowing we lack the tools needed for connecting the two aspects of the world, which presents difficulties to all of us.

But there is clearly more to it than this. Chopra (2010) and others are not valiantly struggling to express connections for which we lack the necessary words; rather, they are enthusiastically leaping into the breach between the two ways and passionately proclaiming a view which has no obvious connection with either the propositional or (in so far as we do have understanding of it) the relational components of the story. There is a sense in which I agree with what they are saying—for instance in the role of cosmic consciousness in our lives p. 127—but it loses credibility unless related to quantum theory as it actually is.

According to Isabel Clarke (2008, 2010), phenomena like this can be understood in terms of the action of a way of experiencing called "the transliminal" (cf. Thalbourne *et al.*, 1997) which occurs when we leave behind the secure but limiting foothold of the propositional. Some of its characteristics are: loss of boundaries leading to loss of a sense of proportion; a sense of mission and unshakable conviction; and a sense of the numinous. Academically, a failure to acknowledge the transliminal at work greatly impedes the study of consciousness and quantum theory, because the extravagant claims and lack of discrimination that the unguarded transliminal can produce brings the area into disrepute.

To counter this we need to keep in touch with the propositional and to recognise the magnitude of the gap between this and the relational. This is why I have stressed the role of modelling in the study of consciousness. We can link a model of some aspect of the relational — in particular, an aspect of consciousness — with our understanding of the physics of the brain, without the danger of being sucked into the uncharted waters of the transliminal.

7.3 Models of spirit

Within the Western traditions a natural source of models of the relational would be those ideas of "soul", "spirit", and so on, which largely stem from Aristotle and have then grown into their fully articulated form. It is worth noting that in later Greek and early mediaeval times a bare distinction between propositional and relational would have been regarded as an impossibly crude classification, compared to the cornucopia of virtues that Aristotle brought into his analysis of the human condition. I will summarise the relevant ideas below, with more details in the endnotes. Aristotle's approach was rational and pragmatic, being similar to that of Teasdale and Barnard, namely seeking to find the most straightforward modelling into parts that was consistent with the evidence available at the time.

He took it for granted that all activities that were not obviously mechanical, including the growth of plants, arose from the working of some non-mechanical component which he called, generically, *psuchē* (soul). In particular, the soul-part of the human could be divided into vegetative, appetitive, and rational souls. The first we held in common with plants and non-human animals, the second with animals, and third was unique to us. The rational soul (to cut a very long story short) is then divided into (at least) two parts, characterised by two different functions.[92] The first (wisdom) is based on knowledge, both practical or "scientific" knowledge and also knowledge of eternal truths, while the second (prudence) is based on thinking things through in order to relate them to "the good". There is an intimation of the propositional and relational here, though the differences are more prominent than the similarities.

Aristotle lists many particular virtues, two of which are particularly associated with wisdom and prudence respectively, namely "action" and "art". Both these conventional English translations of Aristotle's terms are confusing. Action (*praxis*) is not mere "doing" but initiating that deliberate, conscious movement which characterises the rational soul. Art (or "production") is the unfolding of a skill, whether it results in a sculpture or an axe. The following table expresses this. For more detail see [e. 92].

Parts of the (rational) soul	*sophia* wisdom	*phronēsis* prudence
Associated virtues	*praxis* action	*poiēsis, technē* production, art

The meanings of the Greek terms (and, for that matter, the English ones) have changed in the ensuing time, the most notable changes being their adoption into spirituality and theology. In this process their relational aspect has become more pronounced, and they can be seen as examples of the modelling of the relational—either successful or unsuccessful. In early Christendom the most exalted virtue was wisdom, which (perhaps influenced by *hokhmah*, the Hebrew concept of wisdom) became divinised into Sophia with a capital letter, signalling a spiritual entity. The most splendid of Constantine's triplet of churches, started in 360 AD, is dedicated to Sophia, the others being *Irene* (peace) and *Dynamis* (power).

This spiritual elevation of philosophical concepts played an important role until the modern era, alongside the intentional construction of models of spiritual insights. Perhaps its most elaborate and powerful of the latter arose with the development of the Jewish path of Qabalah.[93]

7.4 Praxis

This background leads on to one of the most interesting elements in Aristotle's survey of the rational soul, expressed by the term *praxis*. Literally, this Greek word just meant "action" in Aristotle's time. Subsequently, however, it was adopted into Latin, and the particular role that it played in Aristotle's discussion of sophia got attached to its meaning. So by the thirteenth century in England it has come to mean "direct practical experience… habitual or customary mode of action, method, technique".[94] In modern times the term has mutated further, to mean a form of knowing that integrates practical experience with theoretical analysis. As Carolyn Reinhart puts it, "theory-informing practice and practice-informing theory" (Reinhart, 2013). This concept recognises that academic discourse, with its propositional slant, usually cannot stand on its own. Alongside theoretical discussion, the practical application of ideas is very often a necessary part of understanding them, and it is this practical application that brings the relational into contact with the propositional.

A model of this fusing of theory and practice, spirit and science, is presented by aspects of the eco-spiritual movement, of which my own experience has been with the charity GreenSpirit.[95] This movement (also, and originally, known as "creation centered spirituality") was launched by the Christian priest Matthew Fox (1983), drawing in the work of Brian Swimme (1982) and Thomas Berry (1995). Fox's version of the virtues/activity of being human were represented as cyclical rotation rather than a linearly ascension—a very significant break from the vertical spiritual cosmos of Western thought over the previous two millennia.

Fox's cycle passes through four "ways" (Latin *viae*), characterised as positive, negative, creative, and transformative, as depicted below.

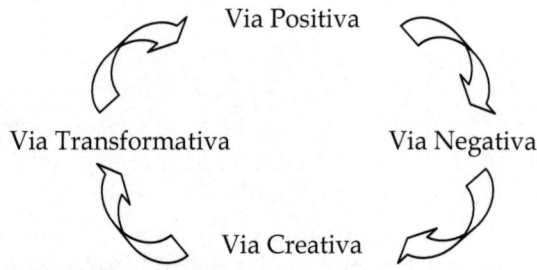

The via positiva recognises the fruitfulness of the universe, its dynamism and splendour, and joyfully celebrates this. It is a path of light that is understood by both the propositional and the relational ways of knowing. But it contains within it the seeds of a more purely relational dark path, the via negativa, that also recognises suffering and death, which must be embraced before the truly new can emerge. This emergence is the via creativa, the inspired out-flowing of pure newness. From this a new phase of the world can be built, standing on the past but transfiguring it in the via transformativa. New fruits spring from this rebirth, returning to the via positiva once more.

This is a cycle that provides a way of looking at all the processes in the universe and in ourselves, from a human being crafting a poem to the destruction of colliding galaxies and their re-formation. It is an alternative way of understanding all our knowing, and hence of understanding all that is known. Most importantly, it breaks away from the linear progression of Aristotelian and Western thought, which dominated our thinking for so long.

This revolution in the basis of spirituality is reflected in a revolution in the concept of praxis,[e, 92] which for Fox takes on a more strongly relational, sensuous quality[96] as well as in the Eastern Orthodox concept of Wisdom, which links with praxis.[97] The four ways describe a new form of praxis which unites practical thought and action (via transformativa) with the silent being of "unknowing" (via negativa) — the ground from which newness can spring.

Brian Swimme's contribution to this way of thinking and knowing was the development of a spiritual response to modern cosmology, and our place within this cosmos. Here the key idea was that of a universe bursting with creativity: there was a constant flux of destruction and creation, as stars died, and then, for larger stars, exploded into supernovae which scattered into space the heavier elements that would birth stars of a new generation that had solid planets. These days one could tell a similar story for whole galaxies, which in the earlier universe collided with each other, destroying their own tidy structures but stimulating a vast burst of star formation.

The biblical image, in the book of Wisdom of the Hebrew scriptures, of Sophia dancing before God in the ecstatic time of the creation of the land, sea, and stars was vastly expanded by Swimme into the expanse of the universe. This creativity then extended to all creatures, including humanity. We are born to create — and we can choose either to do it mechanically, or to do it in the light of wisdom and right praxis.

My own experience of praxis in GreenSpirit stems from the way in which this organisation has built up a living spirituality, connecting propositional scientific understanding with a relational praxis (McCain, 2010). There were many instances where I could be creatively unifying my intellectual appreciation of cosmology, nourished by my professional employment as head of a research group working on mathematical cosmology. I developed, for use within GreenSpirit and elsewhere, my interpretation of the "Cosmic Walk": a conducted walk along a path in a (moderately) natural setting, in which each metre of the path represented the passage of 10 million years of time in the unfolding of the universe. So, as we walked the 1.3 km path, starting with recalling the "flaring forth" (Big Question Mark) where it all began, we recalled in turn the formation of the galaxies, the supernovae that produced the material of our solar system, the formation of the planets, and the progressive stages in the evolution of life. This was praxis in the sense of the action of our bodies as we felt the comparative timescales of these events, as we grew our relationship with the trees and plants that we walked among, and as we shared our experiences with each other. Propositional and relational supported each other.

The question of religion arose naturally. Matthew Fox is a priest, who migrated to the Anglican Church when his own praxis became incompatible with the traditions of the Roman Catholic Church. The members of GreenSpirit were, and are, from a variety of religious traditions: Christian, (neo-)Pagan, Jewish, Hindu... But there is in this community an implicit or explicit recognition that the statements of religious texts are of a different nature from the statements of science, even though we are talking about the same universe.

I give this as an example of a way forward, a praxis, for developing a form of knowing that draws on the wholeness of our being, not separating the propositional from the relational or the mind from the body. GreenSpirit is one particular organisation with a particular focus, but many other examples could be cited of people and communities who are discovering similar paths. They are demonstrating the sort of route whereby we could learn not only to understand consciousness, but to live in awareness of the relationships which form the essence of consciousness.

7.5 Directions for the future

I will now move to a more propositional tone, indicating how one or two of the many loose ends of our exploration might be tied up.

Quantum and conatus

Despite our wide-ranging exploration of different approaches to quantum theory, there is still no definitive solution to three central problems involving quantum theory:
1) How does a single well-defined classically interpretable outcome emerge from a quantum measurement?
2) What are the criteria for a being?
3) How does a being maintain its quantum properties against decoherence?

All these questions call for an integrated propositional-relational approach for their solution.

Question 1 is closest to a solution. We have a number of models of consciousness (§5.4[p. 112]) together with a number of interpretations of quantum theory within which to place them. This open-endedness is essential because a full picture can only come from coupling them with the relational aspect of consciousness. The processes of consciousness, understood relationally, bring to centre stage one outcome from the possibilities presented by physics. The physical situation changes *as if* one of the models described above is implemented. It is in the nature of a model, as distinct from an established theory, that the choice of model is a matter of convenience rather than proof. I have argued that the most appropriate choice for the model involves the use of assertion,[p. 123] with the Hartle's generalised history interpretation[p. 54] of quantum theory.

Question 2 calls for a definition of what beings are conscious; that is, a clear criterion whereby a structure or region[98] can be a seat of consciousness. I have indicated one possible way ahead in the broad criteria of §6.3 ,p. 135 *viz.* unity, quantum properties, and completeness. Of these, "quantum properties" as developed in discussing the "choice of nature"p. 126 is the most important.

The challenge is then to reconcile the requirement for quantum properties with the need to include as seats of consciousness structures such as parts of the human brain that we believe should be conscious: it would seem that a being must actively work to maintain the integrity of these criteria if it is to continue in existence.

A striking form of this action for integrity is expressed by *"conatus"*. This idea in the form developed by Spinoza—the striving of each being to persist in its own being—was introduced in §5.8.p. 126 In relational terms, it is perhaps the clearest expression of the nature of life. We might recall Gerard Manley Hopkins' definitive evocation of this, in his poem "As kingfishers catch fire, dragonflies draw flame":

> Each mortal thing does one thing and the same:
> Deals out that being indoors each one dwells;
> Selves—goes itself; myself it speaks and spells,
> Crying *What I do is me: for that I came.*
> —from Gerard Manley Hopkins, *Poems* (1918)

This central characteristic pins down the core of consciousness. If a being, by its very nature, is characterised by unity and quantum functioning, then *conatus* is the process whereby a being maintains these properties. In terms of the models of consciousness in section 5, we can identify *conatus* as corresponding to the "assertion"p. 123 by each being of these properties.

For example, if in propositional terms we view "unity" and "quantum functioning" as meaning that the seat of consciousness has a (relatively) pure local quantum state, but no smaller part of it has, then this means that *conatus* operates so as to maintain the entanglement of all the parts of the seat of consciousness with each other, as described in the criterion for "completeness" above.p. 137 This could in principle be achieved by asserting propositions which projected onto highly entangled quantum states.[99] The entangled states would give rise to a high correlation (as measured by the covariance) between events in separated regions, producing a system that responded as a unity.

While this might in principle work for smaller beings, when we consider systems of cellular size or larger, it seems clear that a process such as this will be suppressed by decoherence. Our considerations of the whole as a being then suggests exploring the possibility of understanding the emergence of beings through a hierarchical cascading top-down seeding of nested seats perhaps passing, for example, through galaxies, planets, ecosystems, organic life, cells, and organelles. Each region of space that supported a being would manifest quantum properties at two levels: a coarse-grained level at which the region was a subdivision of a being hierarchically higher than it, and a fine-grained level at which it itself developed the quantum mechanical criteria for a being.[100] At the coarse-grained level it would be entangled with other parts of the containing subdivision, while at the fine-grained level it would have its own quantum state.

It seems likely that this will strongly involve the criteria for consciousness, especially the criterion of quantum properties. Starting with the defining consciousness of the cosmic level, each level would through its own *conatus* support the being of subsystems from above. The start of the top-down process would be a pure state of the cosmos as a whole. This process would require seats of consciousness, at each level, to initiate beings based on sub-regions of themselves by first breaking some of the entanglement that the sub-regions have with each other, so that they would have a quantum state localised to themselves. The manipulation of sub-regions in this way could be achieved naturally by the process of assertion already considered.[p. 124] Bottom-up support could involve a seat maintaining its own quantum abilities through its own actions of assertion. It is clear that much work still needs to be done.

7.6 Wholeness

In most sections of this book I have been examining the propositional understanding of consciousness, which has involved the more esoteric details of the interpretation of quantum theory. Alongside this I have, at intervals, placed the relational understanding of the consciousness, which, springing from the notion of panpsychism, has pointed to the fundamental nature of being, from the smallest microbe to the entire cosmos. The gulf between the two ways of knowing could hardly be greater. Then in the previous section I described a particular example of a praxis (not explicitly related to consciousness) which actively integrated the propositional and the relational.

I must admit here to my own divided loyalties. I am fascinated by the elusiveness of a quantum mechanical formalism that is logically consistent and embraces the full range of physical phenomena. In my defence of this, I would argue for the historical importance of taking every lacuna in science seriously, however small: tiny discrepancies in the Newtonian theory of the motion of mercury provided the experimental verification of Einstein's theory of general relativity. So the fact that the explanatory system behind quantum theory doesn't quite add up is for me something that cannot be swept under the carpet. On the other hand, however, I equally acknowledge that at this moment in history the paramount need of humanity is for the opening of our eyes and our hearts to the need for justice for all peoples and justice for the earth—not for refining the details of quantum theory.

I am always delighted when I hear sung the words from a psalm: *"Beati quorum via integra est"* — blessed are they whose way is "whole". "Integra" is full of resonances: uncorrupt, integrated, wholesome, complete. Yet perhaps our splendour, if humanity has any, ultimately lies in the split in our nature, and how we handle it; just as the splendour of the physical universe lies in the "crack" of the uncertainty relation, which forever prevents the universe from settling into dull predictability. It will be for each person and each social group — and perhaps one day for humanity, if it ever achieves a modicum of wholeness — to keep finding out what "integra" is for them.

Synopsis
- The focus of future development lies with the integration of our relational and propositional knowing, at the levels both of the individual and of social structures, particularly religion. Awareness of the pitfalls in the process is essential.
- Traditional models of "spirit" can be drawn on to define the notion of *praxis,* which nourishes this integration.
- Spinoza's *conatus* plays a vital role in understanding the nature of being in a way that links quantum physics with spirituality.

References

Alexander, S. (1920) *Space, Time, and Deity: The Gifford Lectures at Glasgow*, London: Macmillan and Co.
Aristotle (1953) *The Nicomachean Ethics*, trans. J.A.K. Thomson, revised J. Barnes, Harmondsworth: Penguin Books.
Armstrong, K. (2006) *The Great Transformation*, London: Atlantic Books.
Bakhurst, D. & Sypnowich, C. (eds.) (1995) *The Social Self*, London: Sage.
Batthyany, A. (2009) Mental causation and free will after Libet and Soon: Reclaiming conscious agency, in Batthyany, A. & Elitzur, A.C. (eds.) *Irreducibly Conscious: Selected Papers on Consciousness*, pp. 135ff., Heidelberg: Winter.
Beltrametti, E.G. (1981) *The Logic of Quantum Mechanics*, Reading, MA: Adisson-Wesley.
Bergson, H. (1910 [1889]) *Time and Free Will: An Essay on the Immediate Data of Consciousness*, translation of Essai sur les données imméiates de la conscience, London: George Allen & Unwin.
Birkhoff, G. & von Neumann, J. (1936) The logic of quantum mechanics, *Annals of Mathematics*, **37**, pp. 823–843.
Bohm, D. & Hyley, B.J. (1993) *The Undivided Universe*, London: Routledge.
Bohr, N. (1958) *Atomic Physics and Human Knowledge*, New York: John Wiley.
Bomford, R. (1999) *The Symmetry of God*, London: Free Association Books.
Buber, M. (2004) *I and Thou*, trans. Ronald Gregor Smith, 2nd ed., London: Continuum. [Originally published 1958, Edinburgh: T. & T. Clark.]
Cabello, A. (1997) A proof with 18 vectors of the Bell-Kochen-Specker theorem, in Ferrero, M. & van der Merwe, A. (eds.) *New Developments on Fundamental Problems in Quantum Physics*,

pp. 59–62, Dordrecht: Kluwer Academic.
Chalmers, D. (1995) Facing up to the problem of consciousness, *Journal of Consciousness Studies*, **2** (3), pp. 200–219.
Chang, G.C.C. (1971) *The Buddhist Teaching of Totality: The Philosophy of Hwa Yen Buddhism*, Pennsylvania: Pennsylvania State University Press.
Chomsky, N. (1957) *Syntactic Structures*, The Hague: Mouton & Co.
Chopra, D. (2010) *Diving into Pure Potential*, [Online], http://www.chopra.com/articles/2010/02/20/diving-into-pure-potential-by-deepak-chopra/ [14 Dec 2012].
Clarke, C. (1974) Quantum theory and cosmology, *Philosophy of Science*, **41**, pp. 317–332.
Clarke, C. (1976) Reply to Stanley Kerr, *Philosophy of Science*, **43** (4), pp. 583–584.
Clarke, C. (2001) The histories interpretation: Stability instead of consistency?, *Found Phys Lett*, **14** (2), pp. 179–186.
Clarke, C. (2007) The role of quantum physics in the theory of subjective consciousness, *Mind and Matter*, **5** (1), pp. 45–81.
Clarke, C. (2008) A new quantum theoretical framework for parapsychology, *European Journal of Parapsychology*, **23** (1), pp. 3–30.
Clarke, C. (2010) *On the Nature of Bilogic: The Work of Ignacio Matte Blanco*, [Online], http://www.scispirit.com/matteblanco6.pdf.
Clarke, C. & King, M. (2006) *Laszlo and McTaggart – In the Light of this Thing Called Physics*, [Online], http://www.jnani.org/mrking/writings/post2005/Laszlo-McTaggart-Physics-intro.htm
Clarke, I. (2008) *Madness, Mystery and the Survival of God*, Winchester: O-Books.
Clarke, I. (2010) *Psychosis and Spirituality: Consolidating the New Paradigm*, Oxford: Wiley-Blackwell.
Cleary, T. (trans.) (1984–87) *The Flower Ornament Scripture: A Translation of the Avatamsaka Sutra*, Boston, MA, and London: Shambhala Press.
Cook, F.H. (1977) *Hua-Yen Buddhism: The Jewel Net of Indra*, Pennsylvania: Pennsylvania State University Press.
Cooper, D.E. (1997) *God is a Verb: Kabbalah and the Practice of Mystical Judaism*, New York: Riverhead Books.
Coxon, A.H. (1986) *The Fragments of Parmenides*, Assen/Maastricht: Van Gorcum.
Crane, T. (2003) The intentional structure of consciousness, in Jokic, A. & Smith, Q. (eds.) *Consciousness: New Philosophical*

Perspectives, Oxford: Oxford University Press.
Crick, F. (1994) *The Astonishing Hypothesis: The Scientific Search for the Soul,* New York: Charles Scribner's Sons.
Dalal, F. (1998) *Taking the Group Seriously,* London: Jessica Kingsley Publishers.
Dennett, D.C. (1991) *Consciousness Explained,* London: Allen Lane.
de Quincey, C. (2002) *Radical Nature: Rediscovering the Soul of Matter,* Montpelier, VT : Invisible Cities Press.
Descartes, R. (1641) *Meditationes de prima philosophia* (Descartes' Meditations), trans. John Veitch (1901) (q.v.), [Online], http://www.wright.edu/cola/descartes/mede.html [14 Dec 2012].
Descartes, R. (1649) *Le Traité des Passions,* Art 19.
d'Espagnat, B. (2003 [1994]) *Veiled Reality: An Analysis of Quantum Mechanical Concepts,* Boulder, CO: Westview Press.
Dollinger, A. (2012) *Body and Soul* (Reshafim Internet resource), [Online], http://www.reshafim.org.il/ad/egypt/religion/body_and_soul.htm [14 Dec 2012].
Donald, M.J. (1990) Quantum theory and the brain, *Proceedings of the Royal Society of London, A,* **427,** pp. 43–93.
Donald, M.J. (1999) *Progress in a Many-Minds Interpretation of Quantum Theory,* [Online], http://arxiv.org/abs/quant-ph/9904001
de Veer, M.W. & Van den Bos, R. (1999) A critical review of methodology and interpretation of mirror self-recognition research in nonhuman primates, *Animal Behaviour,* **58,** pp. 459–468.
Döring, A. & Isham, C. (2011) What is a thing? Topos theory in the foundations of physics, in Coecke, B. (ed.) *New Structures for Physics, Lecture Notes in Physics,* **813,** pp. 753–941, Berlin: Springer.
Douglas-Klotz, N. (2011) *Desert Wisdom,* 2nd edition, Worthington, OH: Arc Books.
Dowker, F. & Kent, A. (1996) On the consistent histories approach to quantum mechanics, *J. Stat. Phys.,* **82,** p. 1575.
Doyle, B. (2012) *The Measurement Problem,* [Online], http://www.informationphilosopher.com/problems/measurement/ [31 Dec 2012].
Einstein, A. & Born, M. (2005) *Albert Einstein Max Born Briefwechsel 1916–1955,* Langen: Mueller Verlag.
Einstein, A., Podolsky, B. & Rosen, N. (1935) Can quantum-mechanical description of physical reality be considered complete?, *Physical Review,* **47,** pp. 777–780.
Everett, H. (1957) Relative state formulation of quantum

mechanics, *Reviews of Modern Physics*, **29,** pp. 454–462.

Facchi, P. & Pascazio, S. (2001) Quantum Zeno phenomena: Pulsed versus continuous measurement, *Fortschr. Phys.,* **49** (10–11), pp. 941–947.

Ferrer, J. (2002) *Revisioning Transpersonal Theory*, New York: SUNY Press.

Fitt, A.D., Furusawa, K., Monro, T.M., Please, C.P. & Richardson, D.J. (2002) The mathematical modelling of capillary drawing for holey fibre manufacture, *Journal of Engineering Mathematics*, **43** (2–4), pp. 201–227.

Fixsen, D.J., Cheng, E.S., Cottingham, D.A., *et al.* (1994) Cosmic microwave background dipole spectrum measured by the COBE FIRAS instrument, *Astrophysical Journal,* **420** (2), pp. 445–449.

Foucault, M. (2003) *Society Must Be Defended: Lectures at the Collège de France, 1975–76,* trans. David Macey, New York: Picador.

Fox, M. (1983) *Original Blessing*, Santa Fe, NM: Bear & Company.

Fox, M. (1995) Holy impatience: An interview with Matthew Fox, *Yes! Magazine*, Oct 1995, [Online], http://www.Yesmagazine.org/issues/spiritual-uprising/holy-impatience-an-interview-with-matthew-fox

Garden, R.W. (1983) *Modern Logic and Quantum Mechanics,* Bristol: Hilger.

Gerlach, W. & Stern, O. (1922) Das magnetische Moment des Silberatoms, *Zeitschrift für Physik,* **9,** pp. 353–355.

Goddard, L. & Routley, R. (1973) *The Logic of Significance and Context,* Vol. 1, Edinburgh: Scottish Academic Press.

Gould, S.J. (2002 [1999]) *Rocks of Ages: Science and Religion in the Fullness of Life,* New York: Ballantine Books.

Green, B. (2006) [Online], http://map.gsfc.nasa.gov/ [5 Sep 2012].

Griffiths, R. (1984) Consistent histories and the interpretation of quantum mechanics, *J. Stat.Phys.*, **36,** pp. 219–272.

Haack, S. (1978) *Philosophy of Logics*, Cambridge: Cambridge University Press.

Hameroff, S. & Penrose, R. (1996) Conscious events as orchestrated space-time selections, *Journal of Consciousness Studies*, **3** (1), pp. 36–53.

Hameroff, S.R. (1998) Quantum computation in brain microtubules? The Penrose-Hameroff "Orch OR" model of consciousness, *Philosophical Transactions Royal Society of London, A*, **356,** pp. 1869–1896.

Harter, S. (2001) *The Construction of the Self,* New York: Guilford

Press.

Hartle, J. (1991) The quantum mechanics of cosmology, in Coleman, S., Hartle, P., Piran, T. & Weinberg, S. (eds.) *Quantum Cosmology and Baby Universes,* Singapore: World Scientific.

Heidegger, M. (1968) *What Is Called Thinking,* trans. J. Glen Gray, New York: Harper & Row.

Heidegger, M. (1969 [1962]) Zeit und Sein, in *Zur Sache des Denkens,* Tübingen: Niemeyer.

Heisenberg, W. (1927) Über den anschaulichen Inhalt der quantentheoretischen Kinematik und Mechanik, *Zeitschrift für Physik,* **43** (3–4), pp. 172–198. See [Online], http://www.fisicafundamental.net/relicario/doc/Heisenberg1927.pdf

Helfrich, W. (2007) Is the psychokinetic effect as found with binary random number generators suitable to account for mind–brain interaction?, *Journal of Scientific Exploration,* **21** (4), pp. 689–705.

Hemmo, M. & Pitowsky, I. (2007) Quantum probability and many worlds, *Studies in History and Philosophy of Modern Physics,* **38** (2), pp. 333–350.

Inhelder, B. & Piaget, J. (1964) *The Early Growth of Logic in the Child,* New York: Harper.

Isham, C. & Butterfield, C.J. (1998) Topos perspective on the Kochen-Specker theorem: I. Quantum states as generalized valuations, *Int J Theor Phys,* **37**, pp. 2669–2733.

Isham, C.J. (2006) Is it true; or is it false; or somewhere in between? The logic of quantum, in Demopoulos, W. & Pitowsky, I. (eds.) *Physical Theory and its Interpretation,* pp. 161–182, Berlin: Springer.

Itano, W.M., Heinsen, D.J., Bokkinger, J.J. & Wineland, D.J. (1990) Quantum Zeno effect, *Phys. Rev A,* **41** (5), pp. 2295–2300.

Jarosik, N., *et al.* (2011) Seven-year Wilkinson microwave anisotropy probe (WMAP) observations: Sky maps, systematic errors, and basic results, *ApJS,* **192**, p. 14.

Jung, C.G. (1977 [1936]) The symbolic life: Miscellaneous writings, *Collected Works,* **18**, London: Routledge.

Joos, E., *et al.* (2003) *Decoherence and the Appearance of a Classical World in Quantum Theory,* Berlin: Springer.

Kant, I. (1998 [1755, 1781]), *Critique of Pure Reason,* ed. & trans. P. Guyer & A.W. Wood, Cambridge: Cambridge University Press.

Kerr, S. (1976) Many worlds are better than none, *Philosophy of Science,* **43** (4), pp. 578–582.

Klypin, A.A., Trujillo-Gomez, S. & Primack, J. (2011) Dark matter halos in the standard cosmological model: Results from the Bolshoi simulation, *ApJ*, **740**, p. 102.

Kominis, I.K. (2009) Quantum Zeno effect explains magnetic-sensitive radical-ion-pair reactions, *Phys. Rev. E*, **80**, 056115.

Kernaghan, M. (1994) Bell-Kochen-Specker theorem for 20 vectors, *J. Phys. A*, **27**, L829.

Kochen, S. & Specker, E.P. (1967) The problem of hidden variables in quantum mechanics, *Journal of Mathematics and Mechanics*, **17**, pp. 59–87.

Kumar, M. (2008) *Quantum: Einstein, Bohr and the Great Debate about the Nature of Reality*, Cambridge: Icon Books.

Laszlo, E. (2004) *Science and the Akashic Field – An Integral Theory of Everything*, Rochester, VT: Inner Traditions.

LeGuin, U. (1973) *A Wizard of Earthsea*, London: Puffin.

Leibfried, D., Blatt, R., Monroe, C. & Wineland, D. (2003) Quantum dynamics of single trapped ions, *Reviews of Modern Physics*, **75**, January, p. 281.

Leibniz, G.W. (1714) *Monadologie*, §14.

Leibniz, G.W. (1999) Scientiae generalis, *Gottfried Wilhelm Leibniz, Sämtliche Schriften und Briefe*, Göttingen: Herausgegeben von der Berlin-Brandenbergischen Akademie der Wissenschaften und der Akademie der Wissenschaften, VIe Reihe, 4e Band, Teil A.

Li, N. (2012) *Ecumenical Mysticism of Divine Sophia in the Work of Russian Orthodox Theologian Vladimir Soloviev*, [Online], http://www.zygoncenter.org/studentsymposium/pdfs/papers01/symposium01_Li.pdf [10Feb 2012].

Libet, B. (1985) Unconscious cerebral initiative and the role of conscious will in voluntary action, *Behavioural and Brain Sciences*, **8**, pp. 529–539.

Libet, B. (1999) Do we have free will?, *Journal of Consciousness Studies*, **6** (8–9), pp. 47–57.

Liddell, H.G. & Scott, R. (1996) *A Greek-English Lexicon*, Oxford: Blackwell.

Lockwood, M. (1989) *Mind Brain and the Quantum: The Compound 'I'*, Oxford: Blackwell.

London, F. & Bauer, E. (1939) *La théorie de l'observation en mécanique quantique*, Paris: Hermann.

London, F. & Bauer, E. (1983) *The Theory of Observation in Quantum Mechanics*, translation of the above in Wheeler & Zurek (1983).

Marino, L. (2002) Convergence of complex cognitive abilities in cetaceans and primates, *Brain Behav Evolut*, **59** (1-2), pp. 21–32.

Mathews, F. (2003) *For Love of Matter: A Contemporary Panpsychism*, New York: SUNY Press.

Matthews, M.R., Gauld, C.F. & Stinner, A. (2005) *The Pendulum: Scientific, Historical, Philosophical and Educational Perspectives*, Berlin: Springer.

Matte Blanco, I. (1998 [1975]) *The Unconscious as Infinite Sets: An Essay in Bi-Logic*, London: Karnac Books.

McTaggart, L. (2003) *The Field: The Quest for the Secret Force of the Universe*, Shaftesbury: Element.

Merleau-Ponty, M. (1962 [1945]) *Phenomenology of Perception*, trans. Colin Smith (of *Phénoménologie de la perception*), London: Routledge & Kegan Paul.

McCain, M. (ed.) (2010) *GreenSpirit: Path to a New Consciousness*, Winchester: O Books.

McFague, S. (2006) *The Body of God*, Augsburg: Fortress.

McGilchrist, I. (2009) *The Master and his Emissary: The Divided Brain and the Making of the Western World*, New Haven, CT, and London: Yale University Press.

Midgley, M. (2003) *Myths We Live By*, London: Routledge.

Migne, J.-P. (1844–55) *Patrologia Latina*, **175**, Col.0976A. (pld.chadwyck.co.uk).

Nagel, T. (1974) What is it like to be a bat?, *Philosophical Review*, **83** (4), pp. 435–450.

Nagel, T. (1986) *The View from Nowhere*, Oxford: Oxford University Press.

Nicholas of Cusa (1997) *Selected Spiritual Writings*, New York: Paulist Press.

Page, D.N. (2001) Mindless sensationalism: A quantum framework for consciousness, in Smith, Q. & Jokic, A. (eds.) *Consciousness: New Philosophical Essays*, pp. 468–506, Oxford: Oxford University Press.

Park, D. (1997) *The Fire Within the Eye*, Princeton, NJ, and Chichester: Princeton University Press.

Pascal, B. (1662) *Pensees*, [Online], http://www.ub.uni-freiburg.de/fileadmin/ub/referate/04/pascal/pensees.pdf [29 Jan 2013], p. 40.

Penrose, R. (1989) *The Emperor's New Mind*, Oxford: Oxford University Press.

Penrose, R. (2004) *The Road to Reality*, London: Jonathan Cape.

Penzias, A.A. & Wilson, R.W. (1965) A measurement of the flux density of CAS A at 4080 Mc/s, *Astrophysical Journal Letters*, **142**, pp. 1149–1154.

Petersen, A. (1963) The philosophy of Niels Bohr, *Bulletin of the Atomic Scientists*, **19** (7).

Piaget, J. & Grize, J.-B. (1972) *Essai de Logique opératoire*, Paris: Dunod.
Prigogine, I. (1997) *The End of Certainty: Time Chaos and the New Laws of Nature*, Cambridge: The Free Press.
Puri, A.M. & Wojciulik, E. (2008) Expectation both helps and hinders object perception, *Vision Research*, **48** (4), pp. 589–597.
Quint, J. (ed. and trans.) (1955) *Meister Eckhart: Deutsche Predigten und Traktate*, Munich: Carl Hanser.
Revonsuo, A. (1999) Binding and the phenomenal unity of consciousness, *Consciousness and Cognition*, **8**, pp. 173–185.
Saville, A. (2005) *Kant's Critique of Pure Reason: An Orientation to the Central Theme*, Oxford: Blackwell.
Schwartz, J.M., Stapp, H.P. & Beauregard, M. (2005) Quantum theory in neuroscience and psychology: A neurophysical model of the mind–brain interaction, *Phil Trans. Royal Society (Biol. Sect)*, (February), [Online], http://www-physics.lbl.gov/~stapp/stappfiles.html
Skrbina, D. (2005) *Panpsychism in the West*, Cambridge, MA: MIT Press.
Smoot, G.F. (2007) Nobel Lecture: Cosmic microwave background radiation anisotropies: Their discovery and utilization, *Reviews of Modern Physics*, **79** (oct–dec), [Online], http://prl.aps.org/files/RevModPhys.79.1349.pdf
Sogyal Rinpoche (2002) *The Tibetan Book of Living and Dying*, San Franciso, CA: Harper.
Soon, C.S., Brass, M., Heinze, H.J. & Haynes, J.-D. (2008a,b) Unconscious determinants of free decisions in the human brain, *Nature Neuroscience*, **11**, p. 543; & Suppl. Information, *Nature Neuroscience*, **11**, Suppl., pp. 167–168.
Spinoza, B. (1677) *Ethica*, Pars Tertia, Prop. VI, VII, Opera Posthuma, [Online], (Latin) http://users.telenet.be/rwmeijer/spinoza/works.htm; (translation) http://en.wikisource.org/wiki/Ethics_%28Spinoza%29/Part_3 [7 Dec 2012].
Stapp, H.O. (2007) Quantum mechanical theories of consciousness, in Velmans, M. & Schneider, S. (eds.) *The Blackwell Conpanion to Consciousness*, pp. 300–312, Oxford: Blackwell.
Teasdale, J.D. & Barnard, P.J. (1993) *Affect, Cognition and Change: Remodelling De-pressive Thought*, Hove: Lawrence Erlbaum Associates.
Teilhard de Chardin, P. (1956) *La Phenomen Humain*, Paris: Éditions du Seuil.
Teilhard de Chardin, P. (1968) *Science and Christ*, New York: Harper & Row.
Veitch, J. (1901) *Réné Descartes, The Method, Meditations and*

Philosophy of Descartes, Washington, DC: M. Walter Dunne.

Velmans, M. (1996) What and where are conscious experiences?, in Velmans, M. (ed.) *The Science of Consciousness,* pp. 181–196, London: Routledge.

Velmans, M. (2000) *Understanding Consciousness,* London: Routledge.

Von Neumann, J. (1932) *Mathematische Grundlagen der Quantenmechanik,* Berlin: Springer.

Von Neumann, J. (1955) *Mathematical Foundations of Quantum Mechanics,* trans. Robert T. Beyer, Princeton, NJ: Princeton University Press.

Wallace, B.A. (2007) *Hidden dimensions: The Unification of Physics and Consciousness,* New York: Columbia University Press.

Wheeler, J.A. (1981) Delayed choice experiments and the Bohr-Einstein dialog,*The American Philosophical Society and the Royal Society: Papers Read at a Meeting, June 5 1980,* Philapelphia, PA: American Philosophical Society (quoted in Wheeler & Zurek, 1983).

Wheeler, J.A. & Klauder, J.R. (1972) *Magic Without Magic,* San Francisco, CA: Freeman.

Wheeler, J.A. & Zurek, W.H. (eds.) (1983) *Quantum Theory and Measurement,* pp. 217–259, Princeton, NJ: Princeton University Press.

Whitehead, A.N. (1978 [1929]) *Process and Reality: An Essay in Cosmology, Corrected Edition,* David Ray Griffin and Donald W. Sherburne (eds.), New York: Free Press.

Whitehead, A.N. & Russell, B. (1925–27) *Principia Mathematica,* 3 Vols., Second Ed., Cambridge: Cambridge University Press.

Zeh, H.D. (1970) On the interpretation of measurements in quantum theory, *Found. Phys.,* **1**, pp. 69–76.

Zohar, D. (1990) *The Quantum Self,* London: Bloomsbury.

Zurek, W.H. (1981) Pointer basis of quantum apparatus: Into what mixture does the wave packet collapse?, *Phys. Rev. D,* **24** (6), pp. 1516–1525.

Endnotes

[1] "The supreme principle of the possibility of all intuition in relation to sensibility... [is] that all the manifold of sensibility stand under the formal condition of space and time. The supreme principle of all intuition in relation to the understanding is that all the manifold of intuition stand under conditions of the original synthetic unity of apperception. All the manifold representations of intuition stand under the first principle insofar as they are given to us, and under the second insofar as they must be capable of being combined in one consciousness; for without that... the given representations would not have in common the act of apperception, **I think**, and thereby would not be grasped together in a self consciousness" (Kant, 1998, p. 248).

„Der oberste Grundsalz der Möglichkeit aller Anschauung in Beziehung auf die Sinnlichkeit war laut der transz. Ästhetik: daß alles Mannigfaltige derselben unter den formalen Bedingungen des Raums und der Zeit stehn. Der oberste Grundsatz eben derselben in Beziehung auf den Verstand ist: daß alles Mannigfaltige der Anschauung unter Bedingungen der ursprünglich-synthetischen Einheit der Apperzeption stehe. Unter dem ersteren stehen alle mannigfaltige Vorstellungen der Anschauung, sofern sie uns *gegeben* werden, unter dem zweiten, so fern sie in einem Bewußtsein müssen *verbunden* werden können; denn ohne das kann nichts dadurch gedacht oder erkannt werden, weil die gegebene Vorstellungen den Actus der Apperzeption, *Ich denke*, nicht gemein haben, und dadurch nicht in einem Selbstbewußtsein zusammengefaßt sein würden."

[2] „Die synthetische Einheit des Bewußtseins ist also eine objektive Bedingung aller Erkenntnis, nicht deren ich bloß selbst bedarf, um ein Objekt zu erkennen, sondern unter der jede Anschauung stehen muß, *um für mich Objekt zu werden*, weil auf andere Art, und ohne diese Synthesis, das

Mannigfaltige sich nicht in einem Bewußtsein vereinigen würde."

3   http://www.oed.com/view/Entry/39477
4   There is a sort of reciprocal form of the binding problem, namely the intentionality problem (e.g. Crane, 2003). The binding problem is about how the many aspects of our environment, represented in the brain, are brought into a unified experience. The intentionality problem, on the other hand, is about how the many distinct mental qualities of an entity such as the rose are experienced not as being in various parts of the brain, but as being "out there" as a rose. For the paradigmatic case of vision, see Velmans (1996).
5   Kant regards the unity of apperception, the "me", as "the condition of all thinking":

„Dieser letztere Satz [see note 2] ist, wie gesagt, selbst analytisch, ob er zwar die synthetische Einheit zur Bedingung alles Denkens macht; denn er sagt nichts weiter, als, daß alle *meine* Vorstellungen in irgend einer gegebenen Anschauung unter der Bedingung stehen müssen, unter der ich sie allein als meine Vorstellungen zu dem identischen Selbst rechnen, und also, als in einer Apperzeption synthetisch verbunden, durch den allgemeinen Ausdruck *Ich denke* zusammenfassen kann".

Similarly in the earlier paragraph (note 1) he describes thinking as "the act of apperception", using „Ich denke" as a deliberate reference back to Descartes' fundamental starting point.

Saville (2005, p. 55), interpreting Kant, writes: "...I have repeatedly spoken of understanding making its objects something for me. This is effectively nothing other than for me to be self-consciously aware of something as this or that, or to judge it in such a way as I can say to myself 'I think that p' or 'it is to me as if p'." The phrase "I think that p", where "p" would seem to be a proposition, i.e. a thought, suggests that Saville has in mind a thinking-about-thinking, the reflexive aspect of the self. This is much less the case in Kant's text.

6   "conceives" is not in the Latin text.
7   I should note here that many writers ruled out "willing" on the basis of experiments conducted by Libet (1985), interpreting them as showing that what we think is a causal act of will is in fact only the experiencing of an unconscious neural shift that was set up earlier. Libet (1999) himself subsequently explained why this interpretation was invalid, and Batthyany (2009) extended Libet's analysis to the more striking experiments of Soon *et al.* (2008).
8   "Got mvs vil bi ich warden vnd ich vil bi got, alse gar ein, das dis 'er' ynd dis 'ich' Ein 'ist' werdent vnd in dér istikeit ewicklich éin werk wirkent."
9   Sogyal Rinpoche (*ibid.*) speaks of the Master's Rigpa and "The Rigpa of the student", but it is clear that these are two approaches to a view, not that there are two distinct "Rigpas".
10 The subject of this chapter was originally called "quantum theory", when it was cautiously introduced as an idea into physics, but by about 1927 it was being called "quantum mechanics" to indicate that it was now on the same footing as the rest of physics. Now the subject is almost universally accepted as one of the foundations of physics and so I shall, as is usual now, use "quantum theory" to denote the current body of ideas. I will sometimes use "quantum physics" to refer to particular applications of the general theory.
11 Traditional philosophical traditions are famed for their many variations on "being", most notoriously in the case of Heidegger, with Sein, Seyn, dasein, etc. Where it is not simply a participle of "to be", I will mainly use "Being" as a noun with strong associations to the act (verb) of "being", indicating something in which coming-to-be is essential. This is in keeping with one of the derivations of "be" in the *OED* which trace it to the Sanskrit root *bhū-*, interpreting this as "to become" (third edition, "be", outline etymology). I am attracted to this as one sense of "bhur" in the Gayatri. This sense is similar to Meister Eckhart's usage of "istigkeit". This

is "being in itself", whereas consciousness is "being for itself". On the other hand, I will use "existence", with its connotation of "standing out", in a more neutral sense of being-something-or-other; a matter of *what* exists rather than of its essence. Finally, existence as it is perceived analytically loses contact with Being entirely and is seen only as form.

12 Galileo himself did not make this extrapolation from cannon-balls to the solar system, because he knew that fired cannon-balls did not behave in this way (Matthews, Gauld & Stinner, 2005). We now know this is because of air resistance. It was left to the genius of Newton to follow through the passage from the laboratory to the solar system, and beyond.

13 Heisenberg's original "uncertainty principle" (Heisenberg, 1927), which referred to the product of the uncertainties of "complementary" quantities has since been replaced by a variety of stronger principles (see the review at http://en.wikipedia.org/wiki/Uncertainty_principle). In this book I use "uncertainty principle" to refer to the minimum size of the product of the uncertainties of any two variables that are "complementary"; that is, related mathematically in the same way as position and momentum are related.

14 Isaiah. 45.15.

15 Kochen & Specker's argument depended on the fact that in any system there were a great many pairs of quantities that *could* be measured simultaneously without the mutual interference that marked out complementary measurements, and for each pair there was an exact relationship between the results that would be found on measurement. They then showed that it was logically impossible to assign values to *all* the quantities that belonged to such pairs without violating at least one of these mutual relationships. Further details and a proof of this theorem are given in endnote 60.

16 *Local States*. In more mathematical detail (for notation, see note 18) the physical world as a whole, with a system of interest in it, is described (in so far as this is possible, which is not very far in view of general relativity) by the tensor

product $\mathcal{H} = \mathcal{H}_1 \otimes \mathcal{H}_0$ with $\mathcal{H}_1$ describing the system that forms a seat of consciousness and $\mathcal{H}_0$ describing its environment. The Hamiltonian would then be expressed as $H = H_0 + H_1 + H_I$ where the last is the interaction component. We could assume that consciousness can only interact with the system by reference to those states that are significant from a relational point of view. For instance, if $|g\rangle$ is associated with a desirable situation and $|b\rangle$ with an undesirable one, then these would be clearly discriminated from each other, but this would not be the case with $|g\rangle + |b\rangle$ and $|g\rangle - |b\rangle$, for instance. These significant states would need to be fairly stable in most situations if they are to retain their significance, so that they would need to be approximately eigenvectors of H_1 with H_I being small compared to H_1. Given a state $\sum_i \alpha_i |s_i\rangle \otimes |e_i\rangle$ in $\mathcal{H}$ (s in the system, e in the environment) the mixed-state representation of it will be

$$\sum_{i,j} \alpha_i \alpha_j^* (|s_i\rangle \otimes |e_i\rangle) \otimes (\langle s_j| \otimes \langle e_j|)$$

and the corresponding *local state* is defined by tracing out the environmental components to form

$$\sum_{i,j,k} \alpha_i \alpha_j^* \langle e_j|b_k\rangle\langle b_k|e_i\rangle |s_i\rangle\langle s_j|$$

where the $|b_k\rangle$ form a basis for the environment space.

The basic move in decoherence theory (Joos *et al.*, 2003) is now to note that, if the interaction H_I is sufficiently large over a large number of dimensions (a criterion that we also have required, above, for the viability of a conscious interpretation), then the off-diagonal term in the above matrix will average to zero in the k-summation. Thus if the interaction with the environment is large the local state becomes an interpretable classical probability distribution, while if it is small we obtain an uninterpretable (by consciousness) quantum state.

17 Probability theory plays a vital role in quantum theory, so I insert here a sketch of some of its ideas.

Probability, in the modern mathematical sense, is quite a subtle idea that only began to be developed in the seventeenth century. Prior to that, there was either pure knowledge (regarded by Plato as derived from eternal "ideas") which was perfect but hard to access; or opinion, which was unreliable unless you are sure of the sound judgment of the person conveying the information. Probability theory introduced the idea that it was in many cases possible to quantify the certainty that attached to some statements that were neither definitely true nor a random guess.

The paradigm examples of probability are drawn from games of chance, such as betting on dice. If a die is fair, in the sense that there is no difference in its behaviour whichever way up it is, then if you roll the die many times the proportions of the different faces will be nearly equal, and will become more equal the larger the number of rolls that are used. This eventual proportion after many trials is the mathematical concept of a probability. Our expectation that the probability of every face will be the same, and hence that it will be 1/6, is based on the symmetry that exists between the faces.

In the world view of Newtonian physics there is no such thing as probability. The "laws which never shall be broken"[e. 49] of the universe prescribe exactly how it evolves. Probability emerges not because the universe is wobbly but because our information about the state of the universe and our capacities for carrying out the predictions implicit in Newton's laws are limited. Uncertainty arises from our ignorance, not from the universe itself. This is not, however, the case with quantum theory. The Kochen-Specker theorem shows that, within the standard formalism of quantum theory, it is impossible for the universe to have a state from which all possible outcomes can be predicted. Thus uncertainty becomes inherent in the physical laws and is not just a consequence of our own lack of information.

(The later of David Bohm's modifications of quantum theory [Bohm & Hyley, 1993] are consistent with the observations of quantum theory and are locally deterministic. As far as I am aware, however, they have not been shown to be globally deterministic, in the sense that it is still possible that random information may enter the universe from infinity making it impossible to predict future evolution.)

What quantum theory can provide, however, are probabilities for the outcomes of well-defined situations. These probabilities are not based on considerations of symmetry, as in the case of the die, but on the mathematics of the quantum state of the system concerned at the start of some experimental examination.

In all situations except carefully constructed laboratory experiments we are faced both with the intrinsic uncertainty of quantum mechanics and our own partial ignorance of the initial state. There are thus two distinct sources of uncertainty, a situation that is described by a mixed state.

[18] **Definitions to do with quantum space**
(The reader may find a similarity between the following endnote and the endless lists of magical names that wizards have to learn in LeGuin (1973).)

The particular spaces that are used in quantum theory are either complex Hilbert spaces or complex projective Hilbert spaces.

A Hilbert space is like ordinary physical space made up of points but with one special point chosen as an "origin". Any other point can be thought of as defining a line from the origin to that point. Lines (more technically called vectors) have lengths. Two lines define an angle between them, or more generally (and usefully) define a number called the **inner product** which combines information from the lengths and the angles. A line can be multiplied by a number to produce a longer or shorter line in the same direction. The set of all multiples of a given line is called a ray. The collection of all the rays is called a projective Hilbert space. Two lines can be added together by attaching one to the end of the other and joining the end of the former back to the origin to define a new line. The "numbers" used here can be ordinary numbers (as for physical space) or complex numbers—involving the square root of -1—in the case of complex Hilbert space.

Strictly speaking, a **quantum state** is specified by a point in a complex projective Hilbert space; but because these spaces are awkward to deal with one usually regards a quantum state as being a point in a complex Hilbert space, with the convention that two such points related by multiplication by a complex number really represent the same quantum state.

In this book I will call a complex Hilbert space used for quantum theory a "**quantum space**".

While ordinary mathematical notation uses letters (in various arrangements) to denote quantum states (as vectors), **Dirac's notation** denotes a vector by symbols like $|q\rangle$.

Any complex vector space has a **dual space** in which all the numbers are replaced by their complex conjugates (multiplying the part involving the square root of -1 by -1) and the vector in the dual space corresponding to $|q\rangle$ is denoted by $\langle q|$.

The vector produced by multiplying the vector $|q\rangle$ by the number a is denoted by $a|q\rangle$.

The inner product of $|q\rangle$ with $|r\rangle$ is denoted by $\langle r|q\rangle$.

The symbol $|q\rangle\langle r|$ denotes an operator which, when applied to the state $|s\rangle$, yields the state $\langle r|s\rangle|q\rangle$. i.e.

$$|q\rangle\langle r| \, |s\rangle := \langle r|s\rangle|q\rangle.$$

A **mixed state** describes a situation where the actual quantum state is unknown because of lack of information, with only the probabilities of possible states available. Using Dirac's notation, in the simplest case of discrete orthogonal states $|q_1\rangle$, $|q_2\rangle$, ... with probabilities p_1, p_2, ... the mixed state is

$$\rho := p_1|q_1\rangle\langle q_1| + p_2|q_2\rangle\langle q_2| + \ldots$$

The extent of the non-quantum "uncertain uncertainty" in this can then be measured by quantities such as the Von Neumann entropy of the state:

$$S(\rho) := -\mathrm{Tr}(\rho \ln \rho)$$

[19] I derive the metaphor of different *windows* on the world from Mary Midgley (2003, pp. 26–27) who drew the analogy between our concept of the world and a group of people looking into a large aquarium with many windows. The notion of a "sea" of the ultimate comes from the "Ocean of Emancipation" described by Jorge Ferrer (2002, p. 145), a

metaphor in which the variety of faiths and spiritual practices are not paths leading up one mountain, destined to converge, but paths to different shores around this ineffable Ocean.

[20] Later on the day when I wrote this comment, I heard on the news that the Higgs Boson had been discovered!

[21] Using the notation of note 18, the Hamiltonian H acting on a state $|q\rangle$ produces the "state" $i\hbar\,d|q\rangle/dt$ — a multiple of the rate of change of the state, exhibiting the way in which the Hamiltonian governs the evolution of the state. In general, however, the significance of an observable is indirect. If a state $|q\rangle$ has a single well-defined value v of the quantity represented by the observable A (which might, for example, be the momentum of a particle) then $A|q\rangle = v|q\rangle$. The Hamiltonian has a second role of being an observable for the quantity of energy.

[22] "Wave function" and "Quantum state" are more or less the same thing in the case of fairly simple systems: the quantum state of a particle moving in space can be represented as a wave, and the quantum state of a system of several particles can be represented as a "wave" in a higher dimensional space. For more complex systems — such as those involving spinning particles — there is no wave representation.

[23] Malcolm Donald (1999) has developed this idea of many minds in some detail. In the context of this book, the result is similar to combining the principles of selection and generalised histories.

[24] "Remarquons le rôle essential que joue la conscience de l'observateur dans cette transition du mélange au cas pure" (London & Bauer, 1939, p. 41).

[25] "il a *avec lui-même* des relations d'un caractère tout particulier: il dispose d'une faculté caractéristique et bien familière, que nous pouvons appeler la «faculté d'introspection»: il peut se rendre compte de manière immédiate de son propre état" (*ibid.*, p. 42).

[26] "Spukhafte Fernwirkung" in a letter from Einstein to Max Born, 3 March 1947 (Einstein & Born, 2005).

[27] Here and elsewhere I have omitted the normalisation factor $1/\sqrt{2}$ which is normally added to superpositions. The point

here is that, mathematically speaking, quantum states live in a *projective* Hilbert space, whose elements are equivalence classes of complex vectors differing only by multiplicative factors. To do calculations, however, it is necessary to move to the corresponding Hilbert space, while bearing in mind that this is actually too big.

28 It is sometimes stated that when a measurement is made on one partner in an entangled state, the other partner "immediately changes" into having the matching state—even if the two partners are light-years apart. This is, however, too simplistic a view, as can be seen from the fact that "at the same time as" has no meaning in itself, but depends on how the time is being measured. The consistent histories approach to quantum theory (section 2.8) can be modified to give a good understanding of this.

29 The general situation regarding the derivation of the observation process within quantum theory can be illustrated by the example of the 2-slit experiment sketched in the diagram below. The account initially follows von Neumann (1932), translated in Wheeler & Zurek (1983, pp. 549–647).

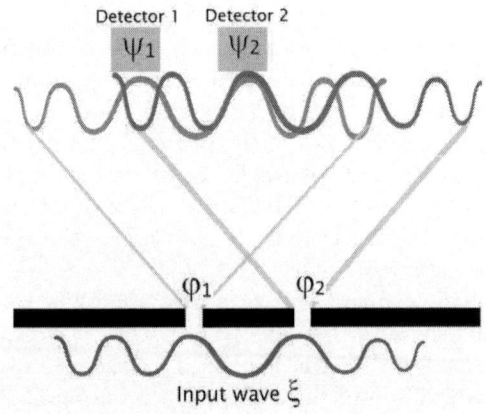

[30] For each performance of the experiment an electron described by a wave function ξ is projected towards a baffle with two slits. The wave function can be separated into a part that strikes the baffle (not shown), and parts φ_1 and φ_2 passing through each of the slits, so that, ignoring the occasions in which no electrons get through and before detection equipment is installed, we have for the (non-normalised) wave function $\xi' = \varphi_1 + \varphi_2$. (As explained above,[e. 27] I omit normalisation factors because only the corresponding projective point is relevant.) The development of the wave function in space is represented by the differently shaded waveshapes depicting the way in which the components corresponding to the two slits interfere with each other, cancelling and augmenting each other in different places. If two detectors are installed at points where cancellation and augmentation, respectively, happen, then (apart from instrumental errors) the first will not register the passage of any electrons, while the second will regularly register electrons (after allowing for those that miss both detectors). This combining to two different possibilities, known as *superposition*, is one of the most distinctive characteristics of quantum theory, as distinguished from classical theory.

Suppose their initial states are ψ_1 and ψ_2. With careful design the back-reaction of the detectors on the electrons can be kept small, so the wave function including the detectors will have the form $\xi' = (\varphi_1 \otimes \psi_1) + (\varphi_2 \otimes \psi'_2)$, where the notation ψ'_2 indicates the state of the second detector after it has recorded the arrival of an electron. The crucial point now is that although this state of the apparatus is a normal quantum state, it appears to the observer as a classical statistical state. The distinguishing feature of a quantum state is its ability to manifest interference effects (as is done in the first part of this experiment) and, more generally, effects dependent on the particular phase relationship between the two components of ξ' above — whether it is as given or whether it is $(\varphi_1 \otimes \psi_1) - (\varphi_2 \otimes \psi'_2)$ or $(\varphi_1 \otimes \psi_1) + i(\varphi_2 \otimes \psi'_2)$ etc. Because, however, these are macroscopic states, extending over comparatively large regions and having enormously large energies compared to single particles, this phase relationship is varying so rapidly that it is inconceivable that it could be determined. If we consider, for example, the energy that a piece of laboratory equipment weighing 1 kg acquires if its temperature increases by 1 degree, the timescale corresponding to the resultant change in the Hamiltonian is $1/10^{36}$ seconds (10^{36} is 1 with 36 zeroes after it). For comparison, the time taken for light to travel the width of an atomic nucleus is, roughly, a tediously slow $1/10^{24}$ seconds — a trillion times longer!

The phase relationship is an "uncertain uncertainty" and the state of the system is therefore described by forming a mixed state and integrating over the circle of unknown phase relationships. This leaves a classical statistical state.

Clearly this effect could be (and is) reduced by careful engineering; but however good this is, it is liable to be defeated by a second influence on the relative phases of the two terms in ξ', namely dynamical changes in the relative phase produced by perturbations from external environmental influences, including gravitational fields and very low energy photons. This has been the main thrust of work following von Neuman, showing that "decoherence" (conversion of the state as seen by an observer to a classical state) is an inevitable consequence of quantum mechanics.

31 When speaking of the initiation of the universe, one cannot refer to a "first moment of time" because (in conventional logic) a "moment" within a continuum is always a point of division or relationship between past and future and cannot be something *in which* something happens. This occupies many pages of Aristotle, Augustine, Kant, and Heidegger.

32 The "re" in the phrase "recombination epoch" possibly refers obliquely to a period even further back in the history of the universe before matter had "separated" from a soup of even more fundamental particles into protons and electrons. On the other hand "recombination" may just be a misnomer that has stuck.

33 In more detail, the fluctuations at the time of decoupling grew because the denser regions exerted an enhanced gravitational pull on the less dense regions around them, drawing matter towards them and so enhancing the fluctuations, which then in turn exerted a steadily stronger influence. Computer simulations of this (Klypin *et al.*, 2011) give a good

match with the overall structure of the universe as we now observe it, with its strands of galactic super-clusters separated by "voids". See http://hipacc.ucsc.edu/Bolshoi/

34 Here is a sketch of the meaning of "consistent" for a history template. Suppose the template M is made up of a sequence of propositions, *viz.*
$$M = P_1, P_2, \ldots, P_N$$
and consider corresponding history outcomes U of the form
$$U = V_1, V_2, \ldots, V_N$$
where each V is either **F** (*false*) or **T** (*true*). Each outcome will then be associated with a probability $\mathcal{P}(U)$ between 0 and 1. First, consider what the situation would be in standard logic. In that case, the proposition "$(P \ \& \ Q)$ or $(P \ \& \ R)$" would be equivalent to "$P \ \& \ (Q \text{ or } R)$" (this is the "distributive" rule). Moreover, if R is "not Q" then $(Q \text{ or } R)$ is always true, so that $P \ \& \ (Q \text{ or } R)$ is equivalent to P. Combining these,

"$(P \ \& \ Q)$ or $(P \ \& \text{ not } Q)$" is equivalent to P. (*)

Similarly "$(P \ \& \ Q)$" and "$(P \ \& \text{ not } Q)$" are disjoint (they cannot both be true) and so the probabilities $\mathcal{P}$ of these satisfy
$\mathcal{P}((P \ \& \ Q) \text{ or } (P \ \& \text{ not } Q)) = \mathcal{P}((P \ \& \ Q) + \mathcal{P}(P \ \& \text{ not } Q)$ (†)
Combining (*) and (†) now shows that
$$\mathcal{P}(P \ \& \ Q) + \mathcal{P}(P \ \& \text{ not } Q) = \mathcal{P}(P).$$
The same argument applies to sequences of propositions or history outcomes, for which (with V_n now playing the role of Q in the previous case and V_{n-1} the role of P)
$$\mathcal{P}(V_1, V_2, \ldots, V_{n-1}, V_n, V_{n+1}, \ldots, V_N) +$$
$$\mathcal{P}(V_1, V_2, \ldots, V_{n-1}, \sim V_n, V_{n+1}, \ldots, V_N) =$$
$$\mathcal{P}(V_1, V_2, \ldots, V_{n-1}, V_{n+1}, \ldots, V_N)$$
(where $\sim$ means "not"). This is the "consistency condition" for histories.

In general, quantum logic is different from standard logic: in particular, the distributive rule used in deriving (*) in general does not hold. So, in quantum theory this result would not be true, and the consistency condition would not hold. It is only when decoherence turns the quantum state into an approximation to a mixture that the consistency condition holds.

The simplest example of an experimental situation in which consistency fails is provided by the Stern-Gerlach experiment,[p. 27] in which magnetically polarised atoms are deflected by magnetic fields. The pairs of rectangles in the diagram below represent the poles of magnets whose field can be oriented either vertically or horizontally, deflecting the atoms either up or down, or left or right. After an initial preparation stage in which the selection of "down" atoms produces a beam with a fixed vertical polarization (corresponding to $V_1 ... V_n$), they pass through two further magnetic fields, the first (corresponding to V_n) deflecting either left (V_n true, say) or right ($\sim V_n$ true) and the second (corresponding to V_{n+1}) deflecting vertically again. Adding the left and right cases to get the total probability for a final "down" result gives 1/2.

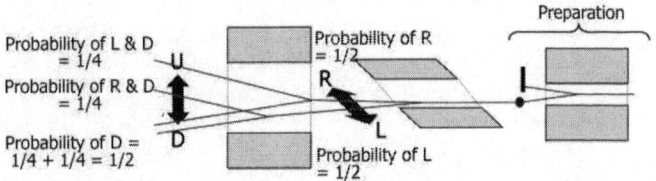

In the second case the intermediate magnet is omitted and the atoms, already prepared to move downward in the vertical magnetic field, give a probability of 1.

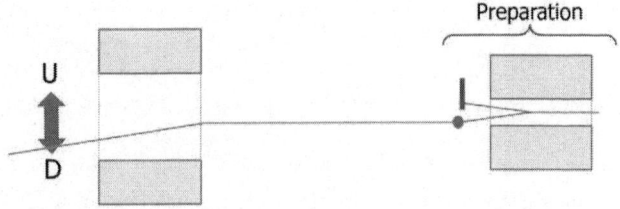

If one were to extend the gap between final magnet and the rest of the apparatus, so that the atoms could interact with the environment which would randomise their spin orientation, then as a result of this decoherence one would obtain equal numbers moving up or down at the final magnet, satisfying the consistent histories criterion.

35 The details of Hartle's approach are important, because it involves a quite different mechanism for decoherence than the conventional approach (§5.2p. 103). The diagram below gives an impression of a generalised history, though some guidance is necessary in order to "read" this diagram.

To begin with, note that the diagram symbolises 4-dimensional space with a Lorentzian geometry, but it is drawn on a 2-dimensional space (with pictorial hints at a third spatial dimension) with a Euclidean geometry. There are three sorts of directions in Lorentzian geometry: time-like (represented below as largely up-and-down), space-like (represented as largely left-and-right) and null (represented as diagonal). The Lorenzian length of a space-like line with a given (Euclidean) length on the diagram gets steadily smaller as its direction tilts to the null direction, the same holds for the time-interval of a Lorentzian time-like line. The time-like and null directions are indicated by the key in the bottom right.

The objects looking like Moroccan tagine pots represent *globally hyperbolic domains*: for each one, it is possible to find a surface cutting across it (there are actually infinitely many possible ones) such that if the physical state is known on that surface then the laws of physics uniquely determine the state in the rest of the domain.

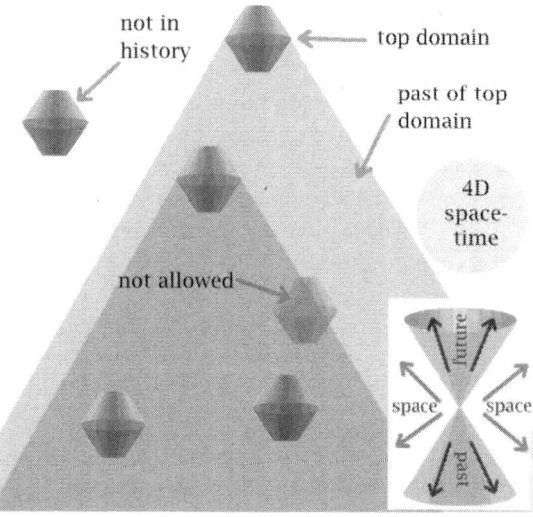

The past regions of two of the measurements are shaded. The defining property of a generalised history is that any two domains have an unambiguous causal relationship: they are either entirely past-future related or entirely space-like related. The "not allowed" domain has parts that are time-like related to all parts of the domain above it and parts that are space-like related to some of these parts.

In a generalised history of the sort defined by Hartle, each domain is associated with a "measurement". In the version being used here, the measurement is part of the awareness of consciousness, and consciousness determines the "window" that defines the measurement.

36 The source of this story, including the detail of each jewel reflecting all the others, appears to be Chang (1971), subsequently more widely and elaborately propagated by Cook (1977). Chang attributes it to *The Flower Ornament Scripture* (Avatamsaka Sutra) but without a functional reference. The closest I can find in the English translation of this Sutra (Cleary, 1984–87) is at vol. 1, p. 368, the passage starting "At that time the Buddha… ascended Mt Suveru".

37 Theoretically it may be possible to construct a model of a particular generalised history outcome, that is, with particular outcomes for each proposition, together with a model of a matching space-time that is correctly modified by these outcomes, and then to apply the procedure for the histories interpretation to obtain a "probability" for this set of outcomes. The flaw with this, however, is that if the outcomes of the propositions were different, then the background space-time would be different, in which case some of the domains that constituted the original generalised history might no longer be eligible for inclusion in this history with different outcomes. Indeed, in a version of the history with different outcomes, in a different space-time, the positions of the domains, or even which domain is which, may not be defined. A history outcome need not define a corresponding history template. Consequently, the "probability" for the original history with outcomes becomes meaningless: it is inconsistent to claim that the probability of a coin displaying "heads" is 1/2 if there is no possibility of displaying anything other than heads. (The concept of a "consistent" set of

histories is essentially a formulation of the property that the histories do produce probabilities that behave properly.)

[38] Here and elsewhere I improperly refer to "time" in cosmology, a concept that is in general not defined in this context because of the structure of general relativity. The symmetrical cosmologies that are considered in the context of quantum cosmology, however, have the property that there exists a unique time co-ordinate with the property that each space at a given time is homogeneous.

[39] „Ankommen, als noch nicht Gegenwart, reicht und erbringt zugleich nicht mehr Gegenwart, das Gewesen, und umgekehrt reicht dieses, das Gewesen, sich Zukunft zu. Der Wechselbezug beider reicht und erbringt zugleich Gegenwart. ‚Zugleich' sagen wir und sprechen damit dem Sich-einander-Reichen von Zukunft, Gewesen und Gegenwart, d. h. ihrer eigenen Einheit einen Zeitcharakter zu."

"Approaching, being not yet present, at the same time offers and brings about what is no longer present, the past, and conversely what has been offers future to itself. The reciprocal relation of both at the same time offers and brings about the present. We say 'at the same time,' and thus ascribe a time character to the mutual offering to one another of future, past and present, that is, to their own unity" (Heidegger, 1969 [1962], pp. 13ff).

[40] In practice one is interested not primarily in the probability that the formalism gives for an infinite sequence of events (such as an infinite sequence of 6s on a die) but with the statistics of particular collections of events (the proportions of 6s as the size of a sample becomes large). Thus the fact that a probability of zero is assigned to a *collection* of sequences in all of which there are more than 1 in 6 6s is a key piece of information. This approach also provides an alternative to the many worlds interpretation which avoids some of the latter's problems. See Kerr (1976), Clarke (1974, 1976), Hemmo *et al.* (2007), Donald (1999).

[41] The duality of the world in relation to our own duality is perfectly expressed by Buber (2004 [1958], p. 15):

"To man the world is twofold, in accordance with his twofold attitude.

> The attitude of man is twofold, in accordance with the twofold nature of the primary words which he speaks.
> The primary words are not isolated words, but combined words.
> The one primary word is the combination I–Thou. The other primary word is the combination I–It; wherein, without a change in the primary word, one of the words He and She can replace It.
> Hence the I of man is also twofold.
> For the I of the primary word I–Thou is a different I from that of the primary word I–It."

42 This refers to my own culinary practices; those of my wife exhibit the cardinal importance of smoothly integrating the two subsystems.

43 Coxon (1986, fragment 7). The first half of my quotation uses Coxon's expansion on p. 191. His literal translation of this part (p. 58) is "And let not habit do violence to you on the empirical way of exercising an unseeing eye and a noisy ear and tongue."

44 Coxon (*ibid.*, fragment 5).

45 Heidegger (1968, p. 215). This is his main discussion of this fragment, building on the essence of *noein* and *logos* described in his *Being & Time* (Eng. 55, D. 59).

46 E.g. "thou shalt see now whether my word shall come to pass unto thee or not" (γνώσει εἰ ἐπικαταλήμψεταί σε ὁ λόγος μου ἢ οὔ—Numbers 11.23).

47 Almost the only thing that is known about information transfer in the brain is that it is mainly carried out by electrochemical pulses travelling along the axons (nerves) that fan out from each nerve-cell. These are like the "bits" which in a computer make up a signal being sent from one part of a chip to another, or make up a document stored in memory. Though we are familiar with these in a computer, when it comes to the brain we don't know how the bits form bytes (if at all), nor what the words are, nor what their grammar is, nor—most vital of all—what their meaning is.

48 "Modum ergo tradere aggredior, quo semper homines ratiocinationes suas in omni argumento ad calculi formam exhibere controversiasque omnes finire possunt, ut non jam clamoribus rem agere necesse sit, sed alter alteri dicere

possit: calculemus." From Guilielmi Pacidii initia et specimina (Leibniz, 1999, pp. 492-93, ll. 22-24).

[49] Praise the Lord: ye heavens, adore Him; / Praise Him, angels, in the height; / Sun and moon, rejoice before Him; / Praise Him, all ye stars and light. / Praise the Lord, for He hath spoken; / Worlds His mighty voice obeyed. / Laws which never shall be broken / For their guidance He hath made (Foundling Hospital Collection, 1796: see http://www.foundlingmuseum.org.uk/collections/.)

[50] Matte Blanco expresses his approach using the formalism of Russell and Whitehead's set theory (A.N. Whitehead & B. Russell, 1925-27). In what follows I am re-working what I believe is the essence of Matte Blanco's ideas in a more modern form. His first principle (Principle I) is that "The [unconscious] treats an individual thing (person, object, concept) as if it were a member or element of a set or class which contains other members; it treats this set or class as a subclass of a more general class, and this more general class as a subclass or subset of a still more general class, and so on." The key word here is "treats": the principle is not a mathematical statement, but a reminder that mental processes are oriented by a particular hierarchical context.

[51] His Principle II is that "The [unconscious] treats the converse of any relation as identical with the relation. In other words, it treats asymmetrical relations as if they were symmetrical." Applying this to the "John is kind" case, his implicit argument is:
- "John is kind" means (in the spirit of principle 1) "John belongs to the set of kind people";
- so from principle 2 we can assert that "[all] kind people belong to [the set of] John";
- which means that John encompasses the totality of kindness.

Matte Blanco sums up this sort of argument in a Principle II_2: "When the principle of symmetry is applied the (proper) part is necessarily identical to the whole."

This illustrates the inappropriateness of the set theory in which he is working. Strictly speaking the above ought to read "When the principle of symmetry is applied the member of the set is necessarily identical to the whole", which is an instance of "circular sets" in which A is a member of B and B is a member of A. A and B can then pull themselves up by their own boot straps, each being defined by the other. This is normally regarded as so outrageous (though it is actually logically consistent) that it is normally outlawed by imposing an axiom to stop it (the Axiom of Foundation).

52 Distinctions between different concepts related to negation become important when the propositional is modelling the relational.

To begin with there are (at least) three quite different concepts related to negation:

a. Logical negation. This refers to propositions and their truth-values. If p is a proposition and we are dealing with two-valued (*true/false*) truth values, then $\sim p$ is a proposition whose value is *false* when p is *true,* and vice versa. In many valued logic, which may include values such as "undefined" or "true from tomorrow", the behaviour of "$\sim$" will be more complex.

b. Complementation. Typically this is context dependent, referring, for instance, to sets of objects within a larger set. For example, in the context of the set of available colours in my copy of the Photoshop graphics programme, "$\sim$508BA4" would refer to all colours having hexadecimal numbers between 000000 and FFFFFF other than 508BA4. The only case where this usage is not context dependent is when the logical model being used has a set representing "everything there is in the world", in which case "$\sim$rabbit", for instance, means "everything in the world that is not a rabbit".

c. Order reversal. This is again context dependent, the context being a quality (or quantity) that can be possessed to a greater or lesser degree. This is often referred to by Matte Blanco in the case of qualities like "goodness". Then the negation of this quality is the quality that simply reverses the ordering (in the mentioned example, "badness"). A typical situation in Matte Blanco's bilogic might be where a given degree of goodness is identified with all degrees of goodness and hence with infinite goodness, and similarly with badness, leading to infinite badness with the scale joining up at its ends into a circle—reminiscent of Jung's concept of "enantiodromia" in which the presence of one archetype evokes the appearance of its opposite.

Matte Blanco introduces early on a general principle of the equivalence of p and $not\text{-}p$ where p is an attribute. He argues for this via a particular case, namely where p is 'x is alive' and $not\text{-}p$ is 'x is dead'. I would claim that Matte Blanco is implicitly using the role of different contexts, and shifting between contexts; indeed this seems to be one of the most important mechanisms that can model the relational subsystem. Rewriting his argument with the inclusion of context-shifts, I would read his argument for the equivalence of "alive" and "not alive/dead" as follows:

"[In a different context] 'alive' and 'dead' might be in the class of 'all possibilities regarding life' and [in yet another context] 'alive' and 'dead' might both be equivalent to this whole class, and hence [equivalent to each other and so] identical."

All this very closely parallels quantum logic, in many versions of which there is no universal concept of negation.

53 "Consequently, when I am at the door of the coincidence of opposites, guarded by the angel [of reason] stationed at the entrance of paradise, I begin to see you, O Lord." From *de visone Dei,* Chapter 10 (Nicholas of Cusa, 1997, pp. 252-53).

54 Matte Blanco claims to be using the version of set theory given in Whitehead and Russell (1925), but in fact he does not respect Russell's theory of types. He also confuses the different senses of infinity (in cardinal numbers, ordinal numbers, and abstract extensions of ordered sets).

55 Many writers have drawn a (loose) analogy between Copernicus's shift of the central point of cosmology from the earth to the sun and Kant's shift of viewpoint (though analogically in the reverse direction) from the world in itself to ourselves as knowers. There is no evidence that Kant applied this metaphor to himself (see http://en.wikipedia.org/wiki/Copernican_Revolution_%28metaphor%29).

56 George Ellis (I think), private communication.

57 Even in mathematics the context affects the truth of a statement. "3 + 4 = 2" is a true statement if the context is modular arithmetic to base 5. In mathematics, however, it is practic-

able to ensure that the context is always explicit—in the case of the above example, by writing the statement as "3 + 4 = 2 (mod 5)"; whereas in natural language the possible contexts are so varied that this is impracticable.

58 The only real exception to this "givenness" of mathematical logic was intuitionism in the original form that was expressed by Brouwer. Following his work, the subject was taken up by Heyting and others and recast within the strictures of conventional mathematics. It is in this latter form that it appears in topos logic.

59 In more detail, the relationship between propositions and geometry is as follows. Given two propositions, such as
A: "the position of the particle in metres lies between 1 and 2" and
B: "the momentum of the particle in kg-metres per second lies between 3 and 4"
then each of these is represented by a plane and the combined proposition
A and B: "the position of the particle in metres lies between 1 and 2 and the momentum of the particle in kg-metres per second lies between 3 and 4"
is represented by the line or (in higher dimensions) by the smaller plane formed by the intersection of the planes for A and B.

An important role is played here by the *dimension* of the quantum space involved, which corresponds to the number of pieces of information, or "degrees of freedom", required to specify the state of the system. For example, in the case of a photon travelling in a fixed, given direction, the photon might be polarised so as to be vibrating in a horizontal direction, as considered from some arbitrary viewpoint, or vibrating vertically, or in some combination of the two (involving complex numbers) giving other linear, circular, or elliptical polarisations. Because two basic pieces of information are required, the quantum space is two-dimensional—the simplest case. At the other extreme, if the system is a particle moving arbitrarily in space it has an infinite number of possible positions and so an infinite dimensional quantum space. This is the usual situation.

[60] Because of the importance of this theorem, I give here a more detailed account of its proof. I use a simpler version due to Cabello (1997) based on Kernaghan (1994) which is slightly weaker than the original, in that Cabello requires at least a 4-dimensional quantum space, while Kochen and Specker succeeded in proving it with only three dimensions. (See above[e, 59] regarding the role of dimensions.)

The proof is essentially a matter of brute force: given a 3- or 4-dimensional quantum space one finds (if necessary by trial and error, but there are short cuts) a particular set of propositions that will deliver the goods, and then shows that it is indeed impossible to assign consistent truth values to them all (if necessary by going through all the possibilities, but again, there are short cuts).

The Kernaghan/Cabello proof sets up the propositions in a 4-dimensional space by choosing 9 different bases (a basis is a set of 4 mutually perpendicular vectors in quantum space — or in general, of as many vectors as the dimension of the quantum space being used). Each basis-vector corresponds to the proposition that the system is in the state characterised by that vector. The significance of bases here is that the set of propositions from a given basis can all be measured simultaneously and the relations between the propositions in a basis is that in any measurement exactly one of them is true and the rest are false.

Each basis functions as a sort of "window" on one aspect of the system in question. The terminology of "windows" was used by Isham and Butterfield, but with a weaker meaning to the idea, noted earlier, of a window on the universe (see chapter 2[e, 19]).

The selection of bases is done in such a way that each basis vector belongs to exactly 2 of the 9 bases. The diagram below shows the relationships between the basis windows, drawn as grey arcs numbered from 1 to 9. The overlapping of two "windows" represents the basis vector that they have in common. Its co-ordinates — four numbers in relation to the 4-dimensional quantum space being used here — are written on the overlap.

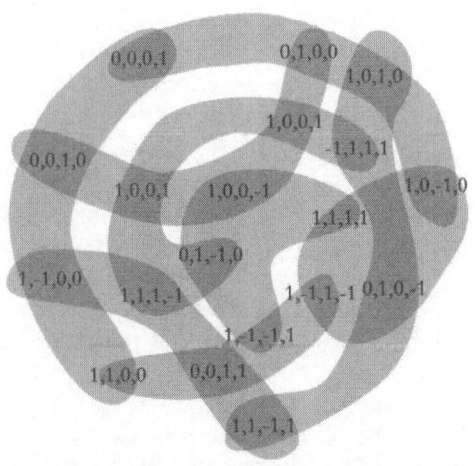

By tracing through the possible values of "true" or "false" for the propositions corresponding to all the overlaps, and using the rule that there can be only one "true" in each window, one soon gets a sense of the way the truth values are interlocked, making it hard to assign them consistently. But there is a neat short cut, as follows. Imagine the windows separated from each other as a collection of 9 separate windows, each with four basis vectors on it (all the basis vectors of the overlaps having been duplicated on the separated windows). Then

1. Each separated window has to have exactly one "true" basis vector on it, so there should be a total of 9 trues in the collection.

2. But each basis vector occurs twice, now that the windows have been separated, and so each distinct vector contributes either 0 trues to the table or 2 trues to the table, so that on that argument there must be an even number of trues in the collection.

3. #1 and #2 are contradictory (9 is not an even number), so it is actually impossible to assign truth values in the way that is required.

To see why BvN logic escapes from this theorem, it is necessary to look closely at the detailed logical operations involved. The key point concerns the intersections of the windows. Take, for example, the intersection of windows 3 and 7 in the proposition 0,0,1,1 shown separately below, with the propositions relabelled by letters.

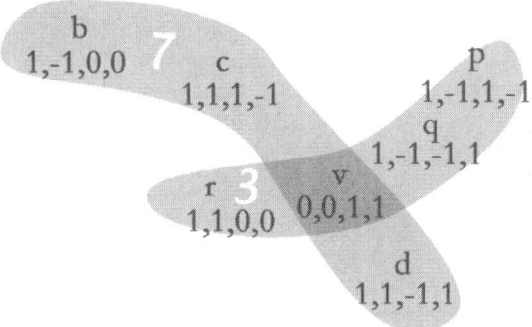

The critical point in the Kochen-Specker argument concerns the relation between the truth or falsity of the central proposition v and that of the other propositions on the two windows p, q, r and b, c, d where, because of the relations holding in each window, the truth of v implies the falsity of all the other propositions. Suppose now, however, that we apply BvN logic to the purely quantum mechanical part of the argument. This means that we will use ordinary logic to talk about quantum logic, a juggling of two logics that would be inconceivable before the 20th century but which is now the bread and butter of formal logic. To keep clear the distinction between the two logics, for quantum logic I will use the mathematical logical symbols: $\wedge$ and, $\vee$ or, $\neg$ not, while I will use verbal description for ordinary logical reasoning based on the geometry of propositions.

The basic relationship in 7 is that
$$\neg\,[\,(v \wedge (b \vee c \vee d)\,)\,]$$
and similarly in 3 that
$$\neg\,[\,(v \wedge (p \vee q \vee r)\,)\,].$$
In other words
$$\neg\,[\,(v \wedge (b \vee c \vee d)\,)\,] \wedge \neg\,[\,(v \wedge (p \vee q \vee r)\,)\,]$$

which implies
$$\neg \{ [(v \wedge (b \vee c \vee d))] \vee [(v \wedge (p \vee q \vee r))] \}.$$
Under standard logic the distributive law would then imply
$$\neg \{ (v \wedge [(b \vee c \vee d) \vee (p \vee q \vee r)] \} \;(*)$$
i.e.
$$\neg \{ (v \wedge [b \vee c \vee d \vee p \vee q \vee r]\}$$
so that if v is true none of the propositions b, c, d, p, q, and r can be true: the truth of any one proposition entails the falsity of six others—a very strong condition that leads to the impossibility of assigning values to all propositions.

In BvN logic, however, the distributive law is not valid, so that the statement (*) does not hold and the proof breaks down.

61 Birkhoff and von Neumann note that every observation of this sort, yielding a "yes" or "no" answer, corresponds to a particular sort of region (a closed linear subspace) in the mathematical space representing all possible states of the quantum system, in such a way that the observation will produce the answer "yes" with complete certainty when, and only when, the state of the system lies in this region. There is another region, entirely separate from the first (the orthogonal subspace) in which the measurement will yield "no" with complete certainty. BvN logic then naturally arises from the relations between these subspaces. The proposition '$p \wedge q$' ("p and q", where these are propositions) corresponds to the region that the subspaces representing each of p and q have in common, and so on. The logic is about the geometry of the space of quantum states of some system, rather than the "state of affairs" of the system.

62 Topos theory (Döring & Isham, 2011) belongs to the branch of mathematics called category theory that tries to unify all the disparate branches of mathematics (such as set theory, group theory, geometry, and so on) into a few basic categories that express the fundamental structures of the theories concerned. Topos theory unifies a variety of different forms of logic, and so it is the natural vehicle for expressing quantum logic.

63 The fact that the same projection can belong to two or more different windows means that windows can overlap (as we saw in the treatment of the Kochen-Specker theorem of note

60). What is more, the overlap is itself a window, so that the windows on a given system form a nested network, as indicated in the diagram below, based on Isham's paper, where the light grey outlined windows are contained in the dark grey ones.

64 Both the interface, if such there is, of quantum theory with conscious beings and the solution to the emergence of structure from a homogeneous quantum state are related to the introduction by Döring and Isham (2011), in their paper "What is a thing?", of "daseination". Both the title and the term echo Heidegger, and indeed his concept of "dasein", the localised being that is the essence of a human, is highly relevant to these fundamental issues of quantum theory. The same cannot be said of the content of Heidegger's "What is a thing?", since in this work he uses "Ding" in a technical sense to denote the reduction of a being to something that is seen only in relation to its human utility.

Döring and Isham introduce a structure that is useful to the extent that it models the way in which the effects of particular existence can be included, in a purely formal way, within the topos approach to quantum; but is says nothing about how this happens from the side of human (or other) consciousness. As I argue here, this stems from relational knowing, not logic.

65 Von Neumann regarded the measurement process as taking place in a physics experiment as consisting of two explicit phases: first, the development of a phenomenon in the experimental apparatus through the operation of the Hamiltonian (which he named "process 2"); and second, the "collapse" of

the state as a result of the measurement (which he confusingly named "process 1"). He specified this latter process as

$$U \to U' = \sum_{n=1}^{\infty} (U\varphi_n, \varphi_n) \cdot P_{[\varphi_n]}$$

(von Neumann, 1955, p. 387), where the φ_n are the eigenvectors of the measurement being carried out on a system in state U, or in Dirac notation

$$U \to U' = \sum_n | \varphi_n \rangle \langle \varphi_n | U | \varphi_n \rangle \langle \varphi_n |.$$

Noting that $U = \sum_{n,m} | \varphi_n \rangle \langle \varphi_n | U | \varphi_m \rangle \langle \varphi_m |$, this means that U' is the diagonalisation of U with respect to the basis defined by the $| \varphi_n \rangle$, producing a classical mixture in place of the original superposition.

66 There is a distinction here between applying will to something in the future, which could be thought to be open to change, on a modern quantum theoretic perspective, and applying it to the past which would react back onto the present. The latter case would be like a magician waving a wand and thereby changing the whole surroundings — which in the case of the Higgs boson would involve altering the entire universe including himself. If, however, it is a matter of choosing between two earlier states *both of which are already known* to be compatible with the macroscopic universe at the time of the willing — as is the case with a current quantum superposition — then there need be no logical conflict.

67 Note that there are two ways of describing what is going on in a measurement. On the conventional interpretation they are equivalent, but the difference could be significant in interpretations that involve consciousness. In the first account, a system is regarded as being initially in a pure state, which is usually an idealisation, because of entanglement.[p. 41] Then on performing a measurement it moves into a mixed state combining the possible outcomes of the measurement with appropriate statistical weights. Consciousness might then be brought in in order to resolve this into a particular outcome. Stapp's approach reverses the order of these steps, with the system starting in a mixed state (the general case), consciousness then restricting the observation to a narrower mixed state specific to a chosen observation, finally followed by "nature" reducing it finally to a single outcome.

68 Explicitly, a straightforward calculation (Facchi & Pascazio, 2001) shows that the expected average time for which the system will be "held" in its original state is T_z^2/T_m.

69 Regarding the effect of decoherence, Stapp (2007) notes that "Because of the uncertainties introduced at the ionic, atomic, molecular and electronic levels, the brain state will develop not into one single classically describable macroscopic state, as it does in classic physics, but into a continuous distribution of parallel virtual states of this kind. Process 1 [von Neumann's collapse process] must then be invoked to allow definite empirical predictions to be extracted from this continuous smear of parallel overlapping almost-classic possibilities generated by process 2 [Hamiltonian evolution]." This does not fit with the actual result of tracing out the environmental variables. In fact Stapp's process and decoherence produce more or less the same results, the only difference being that the latter produces a statistical mixture over *all* the relevant macroscopic variables, whereas Stapp's procedure only does this for the particular variables that consciousness is concerned with at the time. But since decoherence is almost bound to occur anyway, Stapp's process does not add anything to the situation.

70 It would theoretically be possible for events across a system to be co-ordinated within a timescale less than the light-crossing time by having a central signalling device to which the various parts of the system responded after making allowance for the time delays involved, but in the context of organic cells this seems clutching at straws.

71 In more detail, there are two equivalent ways of looking at the measurement time T.
    a. One can suppose that the measurement does take place at a single "time", in the sense that it happens on a maximal space-like surface, this being achieved with some ingenious synchronisation system. Then the transmission of this time into the calculation of the probability of the history is "smeared" by averaging over the hyperbolic domain generated by this surface. Or:
    b. One can accept that the measuring process itself does the smearing of the data.

These are two different ways of expressing what I have referred to as the second decoherence effect (p. 56).

72 In estimating Zeno and measurement times there are very many devils in the details. As noted in the text, shape is important, and for filamentary structures the Zeno effect depends on which oscillatory modes are involved in the interaction with the environment. Some systems can "screen out" interference from the outside to a considerable extent; while co-operative resonance effects can also increase the Zeno time.

73 The idea of (1) a geometrical distortion, produced by a certain amount of mass m, being comparable with (2) the length-scale of its quantum effects can be quantified as follows:

The length $l_G(m)$ of (1) above can depend only on m, G (gravitational constant), and the universal length-time conversion factor (the speed of light) c. It must therefore be given by a numerical multiple of
$$l_G(m) = mG/c^2.$$
Similarly the length $l_\hbar(m)$ of (2) above must be given by
$$l_\hbar(m) = \hbar/mc$$
where $\hbar$ is Planck's constant. Equating these gives as the value for m the so-called "Planck mass":
$$m = m_\hbar := \sqrt{(\hbar c/G)}$$
which evaluates to 2.17651×10^{-8} kg. This corresponds to Penrose's "1 graviton" criterion. On the other hand a microtubule of typical dimensions length = 25 µm and diameter 25 nm will have a mass of about 3×10^{-17} kg.

74 There is a correspondence between intuitionism and an aspect of topos logic. Intuitionism generalises normal logic by introducing the idea of "stages of truth": truth is not a timeless absolute, but something that is actively and progressively realised (perhaps in a context dependent way, though that is not made explicit) in the historical process of mathematics. Logic evolves. Similarly, in Isham's concept of windows above[e, 63] a succession of larger windows (a logical succession known as a "seive") can progressively increase the range of propositions to which a truth-value can be applied, again producing stages of truth. Topos theory describes

purely logical aspects of this, stripped of the context of propositions, quantum theory, and so on.

[75] (For notation, see note 18.) We can compare the process of assertion with Stapp's process of using the Zeno effect to shift the state of the brain into a mixture of a state where a desired outcome occurs and one where its negation occurs. To do this, consider an initial state $|I\rangle$ of the form
$$|I\rangle = a|A\rangle + \beta|B\rangle$$
where $|\beta|^2 = 1 - |a|^2$. Then the mixed state representing the result of applying a projection on $|A\rangle$ as a measurement is
$$|a|^2|A\rangle\langle A| + |\beta|^2|B\rangle\langle B|$$
whereas the mixed state from asserting $|A\rangle$ is
$$|a|^2(1+|\beta|^2)|A\rangle\langle A| + a\beta^*|\beta|^2|A\rangle\langle B| +$$
$$a^*\beta|\beta|^2|B\rangle\langle A| + |\beta|^4|B\rangle\langle B|$$
(where * denotes complex conjugate).

Both the conventional Zeno process and assertion can be used to move the state into a particular state (e.g. $|A\rangle$ in the example above). For this the conventional process must be modified as follows. A measurement of projection on $|A\rangle$ is repeated at intervals of the Zeno time T_z until the result is "true"; thereafter a measurement is repeated at intervals of the measurement time T_m in order to hold it in position. This is an extension of Stapp's method, the latter leaving it to "nature" to select, to select a particular outcome. The timescale of this modified Zeno process is the Zeno time, while that of assertion is faster, being governed by the measurement time.

[76] PROPOSITIO VI. Unaquaeque res, quantum in se est, in suo esse perseverare conatur.
DEMONSTRATIO. Res enim singulares modi sunt, quibus Dei attributa certo et determinato modo exprimuntur (per coroll. prop. 25. P. 1.), hoc est (per prop. 34. P. 1.) res, quae Dei potentiam qua Deus est et agit, certo et determinato modo exprimunt. Neque ulla res aliquid in se habet, a quo possit destrui, sive quod eius existentiam tollat (per prop. 4. huius); sed contra ei omni, quod eiusdem existentiam potest tollere, opponitur (per prop. praeced.). Adeoque quantum potest et in se est, in suo esse perseverare conatur. Q.E.D.

PROPOSITIO VII. Conatus, quo unaquaeque res in suo esse perseverare conatur, nihil est praeter ipsius rei actualem essentiam.

DEMONSTRATIO. Ex data cuiuscumque rei essentia quaedam necessario sequuntur (per prop. 36. P. 1.), nec res aliud possunt, quam id quod ex determinata earum natura necessario sequitur (per prop. 29. P. 1.). Quare cuiuscumque rei potentia sive conatus, quo ipsa vel sola vel cum aliis quidquam agit, vel agere conatur, hoc est (per prop. 6. huius) potentia sive conatus, quo in suo esse perseverare conatur, nihil est praeter ipsius rei datam sive actualem essentiam. Q.E.D.

77 The idea that we have three "eyes" — the eye of the flesh, the eye of reason, and the eye of contemplation — comes from Hugh of St Victor, 1096–1141 (Migne, 1844–55):

"Est autem oculus triplex: oculus carnis, oculus rationis, oculus contemplationis. Oculus carnis apertus est, oculus rationis lippus, oculus contemplationis clausus et caecus. Oculo carnis videtur mundus, et ea quae sunt in mundo. Oculo rationis animus, et ea quae sunt in animo. Oculo contemplationis Deus, et ea quae sunt in Deo."

"Now, the eye is threefold: the eye of the flesh, the eye of reason, the eye of contemplation. The eye of the flesh is open, the eye of reason bleary, the eye of contemplation closed and blind. The eye of the flesh sees the world and what is in the world, the eye of reason the spirit and what is in the spirit, the eye of contemplation God and what is in God."

The concept is, however, usually attributed to St Bonaventure, although he cites it with due acknowledgment!

78 The word "being" not only functions as both a verbal participle and a noun, but it also means the property of existence, and Being — with a capital — is the standard usage for this property considered as an entity in itself.

79 cf. Martin Buber's (2004) "He is a 'thou' and fills the heavens."

80 For an example of incidental nesting, if we were to decide that the very widely occurring mammalian parasite *toxoplasma gondii* was at a primitive level conscious, and also that the seat of human consciousness was a largish part of the brain, then about 2 billion people will be harbouring these

alien seats of consciousness within their own seat of consciousness, without it contributing in the slightest to their consciousness itself.

[81] The case of the Black Cloud raises more complex issues. The electromagnetic field that connects the particles of the Cloud is presumed to be classical, but in the case of this field the classical picture and the quantum picture are less sharply separated. It seems appropriate to postpone the consideration of this more complex case.

[82] Sometimes quantum theory is contrasted with classical physics, with the latter being described as "mechanical", regarding its entities as like a machine in the sense that it is large, solid, permanent, and predictable; whereas the entities in quantum physics have few of these attributes. Here, however, I am using it (improperly, I admit) to indicate its propositional character and to distinguish its action from the action of be-ing.

[83] The idea of the strength of an entanglement in more detail is as follows (Clarke, 2007, p. 74). Let $|S\rangle$ denote a state in a tensor product of Hilbert spaces H_A and H_B corresponding to two different spatial regions. Define

$D(S, H_A, H_B) = \sup_{P,Q} 4 \left(\langle S | P | S \rangle \langle S | Q | S \rangle - \langle S | PQ | S \rangle \right)$

where S is a quantum state on $P \otimes Q$, P, Q range over projections on H_A and H_B (and their negations) and we identify P with $P \otimes I_B$ acting on $H_A \otimes H_B$ and similarly for Q. Then the quantity

$$\langle S | P | S \rangle \langle S | Q | S \rangle - \langle S | PQ | S \rangle$$

above is just the statistical covariance between P and Q, so that D is a measure of the maximum attainable magnitude for this correlation, normalised to lie between 0 and 1. $D = 0$ when and only when $|S\rangle$ is unentangled (factorisable) and for given H_A and H_B the state

$$|S\rangle = \frac{1}{\sqrt{2}} \left(u^A \otimes v^B \pm v^A \otimes u^B \right)$$

achieves $D = 1$. A general definition of "coherence" would then be that D was exceptionally high.

[84] My original specification of this idea of defining a being in terms of entanglement did not, however, sufficiently take into account either quantum cosmology or the distinction

between the relational and the propositional ways of knowing. It was largely based on the conventional view of quantum theory that takes for granted the highly evolved and differentiated universe in which we live, in which it is reasonable to divide things up into "systems", "observers", "apparatus", "particles", and so on. From this standpoint, every large system is subject to decoherence (§2.6[p. 37]) that wipes out quantum effects and gives the universe around us the properties that are the subject of classical physics. Decoherence effectively limits discernable quantum effects to very small systems and thus limits the scope for representing consciousness as a quantum process. As this approach has dominated writing about the quantum–consciousness connection for many years, I will describe it in more detail.

Suppose that a system—that is, some clearly defined region containing physical object(s) of interest—is in a particular, known, pure quantum state. This might result either because an external observer contrives such a state, or because of some sort of action of consciousness. In general such a state will be coherent (see [e. 83]), with strong *internal* correlations between what happens in any two distinct parts of the system. From the moment that this state is set up, however, the system starts interacting with the whole of the universe around it, resulting in its becoming *externally* entangled in minutest detail with all the rest of the universe. An observer standing outside the system has no way whatever of knowing any of these details. So as far as this observer is concerned, the effect of this entanglement can only be represented as a collection of probabilities applied to the system, represented by the mathematical process of "tracing out" the unknown entanglements. This turns the state of the system into a "mixed state" that incorporates both the uncertainty arising from the net effect of the universe and the state of the system, removing the coherence that was originally present. As this mixed state evolves, at a rate that depends on the size of the system (the larger the faster), the *quantum* uncertainty that is inherent in the system itself is obliterated along with its coherence, leaving only probabilities. This is the mechanism of *decoherence* whereby the classical world emerges from the unknown entanglement of the system with the surrounding universe.

[85] Only a few aspects of Whitehead's God are relevant here: notably the concept of an "actual entity" (our "Being"), the fact that God is essentially open to change, and the necessary combining of subject and superject at all levels. Cosmos is, however, obviously on a lower level than God, even Whitehead's God, in having physical structure.

[86] "A l'inverse des « primitifs » qui donnent un visage à tout ce qui bouge, — ou même des premiers Grecs, qui divinisaient toutes les faces et toutes les forces de la Nature, l'Homme moderne est obsédé par le besoin de dépersonnaliser (ou d'impersonnaliser) ce qu'il admire le plus. Deux raisons à cette tendance. La première est l'Analyse, — ce merveilleux instrument de recherche scientifique, auquel nous devons tous nos progrès, mais qui, de synthèse en synthèse dénouées, laisse échapper l'une après l'autre toutes les âmes, et finit par nous laisser en présence d'une pile de rouages démontés et de particules évanescentes. — Et la seconde est la découverte du monde sidéral, objet tellement vaste que toute proportion paraît abolie entre notre être et les dimensions du Cosmos autour de nous. — Capable de réussir et de couvrir à la fois cet Infime et cet Immense, une seule réalité semble subsister : l'Énergie, entité flottante universelle, d'où tout émerge, et où tout retombe, comme dans un Océan. L'Énergie, le nouvel Esprit. L'Énergie, le nouveau Dieu. A l'Oméga du Monde, comme à son Alpha, l'Impersonnel" (Teilhard de Chardin, 1956, p. 177).

[87] In the usual editions the pensée "Le silence éternel de ces espaces infinis m'effraie" is preceded by "Toute notre dignité consiste donc en la pensée. C'est de là qu'il nous faut relever et non de l'espace et de la durée, que nous ne saurions remplir. Travaillons donc à bien penser voilà le principe de la morale" (Pascal, 1662). This evidences a stark dichotomy between humans' capacity for thought and the sterility of the material universe. Teilhard is considerably more optimistic, in regarding Christ as a "universal element" in the universe, and in works after *The Phenomenon of Man,* such as *Science and Christ,* supplementing the inert "energy" of the former

88 Abrahamic traditions here differ strikingly from Eastern and indigenous ones, and particularly with later Theravada Buddhism. The monotheism of the former places ultimate reality outside the physical world, while the latter tends to shift the emphasis away from a fixed absolute and towards basic dynamic principles such as dependent co-arising.

89 יְהִי רָקִיעַ בְּתוֹךְ הַמָּיִם, וִיהִי מַבְדִּיל, בֵּין מַיִם לָמָיִם. See on this Douglas-Klotz (2011, p. 68).

90 The Easter Vigil, a long rite taking place at night on the day before Easter, consists of a number of readings in which the parting of the waters of the Red/Reed Sea must be included, followed by the kindling of new fire and lighting of engraved candles, and by the blessing of the waters of the font. This may be followed by baptisms: originally this was the only day on which baptisms could be performed. Jung (1977 [1936], p. 158) describes the symbolism of the blessing of the font, including the moment when the priest "divides the water in the fourfold form of the cross". Jung places this ritual in the category of religious initiations which seal a human being's passage from a child psychically dependent on its parents to the status of full autonomy: the moment when a composite is divided so that a new being is liberated.

91 Note that Buber (like Heidegger—see e. 64) uses "thing" in a pejorative sense, as referring to an "It" rather than a "Thou".

92 I will here draw on Aristotle's treatment in the *Nicomachean Ethics* (Aristotle, 1953), all references in this section using the "Bekker numbers" of this book. The emphasis here is on the practical question of the moral aims and actions of humans, though the model that is built up is more generally relevant.

The rational soul is effectively divided into two parts (1143b15) distinguished by their two distinct functions of prudence (*phronēsis*) and wisdom (*sophia*). Phronēsis is the faculty of thinking forward practically, through to the final goal of acting for good (1140a25ff), while sophia is a combination of the knowledge of the way things are (*epistēmē*) and the intuition (*nous*) of ultimate ends (1141b2). Aristotle says of the wise person that they "must not only know all that follows from the first principles, but must also have a true understanding of those principles. Therefore wisdom must be intuition *and* scientific knowledge" (1141a18).

Associated, respectively, with sophia and phronēsis are action (*praxis*) and production or art (*poiēsis*) — although the person who reaches perfection in the arts has gone beyond the bounds of art itself and manifests sophia (1141a10).

For Aristotle, *praxis* meant deliberate, purposive action, which is seen as being alongside the attainment of truth. Such action requires choice, and choice involves appetition and purposive reasoning, together with a certain moral state (1139a32). Thus the human virtues of antiquity tend to bring together strands which we would now separate into practical and spiritual.

Carolyn Reinhart (2013, p. 9) characterises praxis as "theory-informing practice and practice-informing theory", remarking that "With such a dynamic flow back and forth, we are on a journey of growth, change, and hopefully transformation." Similarly Josie Gregory (private paper) writes that "Phronesis is a form of action which does not have a purpose outside itself. It is a matter of conduct, a matter of doing, rather than of making. For example, making money has an aim distant from the act of making money, whereas in 'the doing' (phronesis) the end cannot be other than the act itself; doing good is an end in itself. Phronesis can only come from praxis, from a disposition that is post-reflexive, that is, a higher reasoning capacity that perceives the inherent essence of action."

[93] In the Judaic tradition Sophia was frequently identified with the Qabalistic sefer Hokhmah which, in parallel with Binah (understanding) formed the highest level below the ultimate source of Ein Sof.

Perhaps it is not too fanciful to borrow these sefirot for a top layer of Aristotle's analysis, as in the following table:

Binah (understanding)	Hokhmah (divine wisdom)
↑	↑
phronēsis (discerning thought)	sophia (eternal wisdom)
↑	↑
poiēsis (grounded action)	theoria (vision)

94 *Oxford English Dictionary*, 3rd edition, March 2007.
95 http://www.greenspirit.org.uk/
96 "Wisdom is always taste—in both Latin and Hebrew, the word for wisdom comes from the word for taste—so it's something to taste, not something to theorize about. 'Taste and see that God is good,' the psalm says; and that's wisdom: tasting life. No one can do it for us. The mystical tradition is very much a Sophia tradition. It is about tasting and trusting experience, before institution or dogma" (Fox, 2005).
97 "Ecumenical ideas for Soloviev were never just a theory but his active Christian praxis, the meaning for his life and the essence of his creative work... In Russian Orthodox spirituality, the understanding of the beauty of Divine Sophia as God's Wisdom and the Church is profound" (Li, 2012).
98 In more detail: it seems appropriate to define which things are conscious in two stages. First we specify the coarsest level of what a "thing" is. We could start with simply a region of space (or space-time) and all of its content, but the problem here is that we could, at least in theory, have more than one being occupying the same region. For instance, one might be based on electromagnetic fields and metallic conductors and another based on chemical interactions using non-conducting fluids and channels. So the most appropriate coarse specification might entail a region *and* a Hilbert space representing the dynamics in that region. Different things in the same region would have different Hilbert spaces, and the total Hilbert space in the region would contain as factors all the coarse-thing spaces.
99 The following is an explicit, though entirely arbitrary, illustration of how internal entanglement within a seat of consciousness could be maintained. Suppose that on anatomical grounds we decompose the total Hilbert space of a being into the tensor product $\mathcal{H} = \mathcal{H}_1 \otimes \mathcal{H}_2 \otimes ... \otimes \mathcal{H}_n$ where the component Hilbert spaces correspond to disjoint regions of the seat, and that each $\mathcal{H}_k$ is split into the Cartesian sum $\mathcal{H}_k = U_k + V_k$ of orthogonal subspaces, with P_k the projection on V_k. Then from note[e. 82] we can see that by asserting projections of the form $(1/\sqrt{2})(P_k \otimes P_l + [I - P_k] \otimes [I - P_l])$ for a variety of pairs (k, l) we can increase the measure of entanglement (covariance) D.

[100] The coarse/fine-grained distinction in quantum theory is often overlooked. When talking about the quantum state of, for instance, a molecule it might be implicitly understood that the atoms in the molecule would be regarded as basic particles with quantum properties within the molecule depending only on their mass, charge, and spin. At a finer grading, however, these atoms would be decomposed into systems in their own right, with quantum properties based on a nucleus and electrons... and so on, down to whatever is regarded as the "fundamental" level of physics (currently quarks, bosons, and so on).

Index

A
action. *See* praxis
alētheia. *See* truth
Alice, 24, 58
apparatus. *See* measurement
apperception, 6, 7, 12
Aristotle, 76, 79, 86, 93, 149
   praxis & ethical categories, e92: 204
Armstrong, 74, 76
assert, 73, 90
assertion, 123–5, 138, 158
   compared with Zeno, e75: 199
association, 84

B
baptism, 142
   division of waters, 142, e90: 204
Barnard. *See* Teasdale & Barnard
bat. *See* Nagel
being, 19, 141
   nature of the word, e11: 171
Bergson, 61
big bang. *See* Big Question Mark
Big Question Mark, 47, 49, 52, 142, 154
bilogic, 85, *See also* Matte Blanco
binding problem, 10
Birkhoff, 92, 94, 96
   & von Neumann, logic & geometry, e61: 194
body, 5, 8, 14, 17, 72, 154
   memory stored in, 129
   of God, 142
Bohr, 26, 64, 77, 116, 140
Buber, world is twofold, e41: 185
Buddhism, 18
Buddhist, 19
Butterfield. *See* Isham

C
certainty, 87, *See also* uncertainty
Chalmers, 9, 10
Christian tradition, 19, 72, 142, 152
Clarke, Isabel, 148
coarse graining, 98, e100: 207
cognitive subsystems. *See* Teasdale & Barnard
coherence. *See also* decoherence
   of knowing, 13, 104–7
collapse (interpretation), 37, 45, 50, 53, 97, 105, 122, 123
completeness, 137, 157

conatus, 128, 138, 155, 156
  Spinoza on, e76: 199
conceive, 16
noein, 73
conceptual. *See* non-conceptual
consciousness, 2
  See also epiphenomenalism, McGilchrist, Teasdale & Barnard, Wheeler
  cosmic, 18, 19, 50, 132
  definition of, 4, 9, 10
  hierarchical, 123
  models of, 109, 112
  operation of, 103
  other than human, 14, 39, 135
  seat of, 14, 105, 107
  simplicity of, 20
  subjective, 11, 13, 70
  subjective study of, 18
  what it does, 19–22, 101, 107, 112, 113, 127–32, 160–7
  will, 16
context. *See* logic, context in
cosmology, 46, 58
  expansion, 47
  quantum, 46, 49, 50, 56, 60
  radiation, microwave, 47, 48
cosmos, 139
  & God, 142
  & quantum, 56
  & Teilhard, 142
  & Whitehead, 141
  as a being, 140
  as treacle well, 58
  consciousness of, 157
  observations, 48
  quantum observation of, 59
  quantum state of, 127
  self-observation, 52
  structure formation, 48, 49
  our place in, 153
  vertical spirituality, 152
  view from nowhere, 140
crack in everything, 159
creation
  & God, 153
  making a division, 142
  spirituality, 151
  Wheeler, 40

D

d'Espagnat, 64
decoherence, 44, 46, 53
  blocking quantum consciousness, e84: 201
  second source of, 56
  Stapp's view 15, e69: 197
Dennett, 8, 108
Descartes, 5, 8
  & will, 16
division of waters. *See* baptism
Donald, 60

E

Eckhart, Meister, 19, 20, 127, 132
  work of God, 19
Einstein, 26
  spooky action, 42
  vs. Bohr, 77, 140
entanglement, 40, 41, 44
  & Beings, 157
  & mixed state, 45, 106
  & seat of consciousness, 137
  & unity, 137
  definition of strength of, e83: 201
  maintained by consciousness, e98: 206

not simultaneous, e28: 178
environment
   & decoherence, 43, 104
   & Zeno effect, 119
epiphenomenalism, 107
Everett, 37
evolution, 81, 109, 118
   Hamiltonian, 116
   of cosmos. *See* cosmos, structure
   vs. *conatus*, 129
eye of the spirit, 2, 132
   Hugh of St Victor on, e77: 200

F
Ferrer, 143
   Ocean of Emancipation, e19: 176
field, 34–5
   & Beings, 135
fluctuations
   & measurement, 50
   growth after decoupling, e33: 180
   in microwave radiation, 48
   quantum, 49, 51, 60
Foucault, Michel, 68
   & knowing, 79
fourfold division of mind, 78, 146
Fox, Matthew, 152, 154

G
Galileo
   extrapolation from experiment, e12: 172
generalised histories, 55, 56, 62, 103
   diagram of, e35: 183
God, 19
   as observer, 50
   beyond cosmos, 142
   body of, 142
   creation, 153
   isness, 132
   logos, 74
   problematic, 147
   Whitehead's, 141
   work of, 127
Goddard, 89
Gould, magisteria, 147
gravity & quantum collapse (Penrose), e73: 198
GreenSpirit, 151, 153

H
Hameroff
   & Penrose, model, 121, 138
   seat of consciousness, 107
Hamiltonian, 31
   & generalised histories, 103
   based on operators, 35
   for Stapp, 116
hard problem, 9
Hartle, 54, 55
   combining with Page etc., 62
   history as model for *conatus*, 129
Hebrew tradition, 72, 74, 142
   & Wisdom, 150, 153
Heidegger
   & truth, 76
   four-dimensional time, 61
   three-dimensional time, e39: 185
   Parmenides & logic, 73
Heisenberg
   matrices, 31
   uncertainty relations. *See* uncertainty
hierarchy. *See* consciousness, hierarchical

histories interpretation, 53, 54
  generalised. *See* generalised histories
  consistent, definition, e34: 181
history template/outcome, 54
Hopkins, 156
Hoyle
  steady state theory, 47
  The Black Cloud, 135

I
"I", 12, *See also* 'me'
intentionality problem, e4: 170
interpretations of quantum theory, 23, *See also* quantum
intuitionism
  & topos logic, e74: 198
  Brouwer vs. Heyting, e58: 190
Isham, 92
  eggs & sausage, 94
  topos logic, 96

J
Jung, division of waters. *See* baptism

K
Kant, 6
  & binding, 10
  & Eckhart, 20
  & self-consciousness, 13
  apperception & 'me', e5: 170
  copernican shift, 87
  sensibility & intuition, e1: 169
  unity of consciousness, e2: 169
knowing
  & being, 63
  & being, in Eckhart, 20
  & Platonic world, 32
  & quantum contexts, 64
  inception of formal logic, 76
  logos & *noein*, 75
  reinvention of, 67
  relational & propositional, 2, 20, *See also* Teasdale & Barnard
  subjective or shared, 2
  subjugated (Foucault), 68
  through relationship, 61
Kochen-Specker theorem, 26
  & alternative logic, 93
  & reality, 106
  & uncertainty, 27, 29
  proof of, e60: 191

L
legein. See assert
Leibniz, "Let us calculate", e48: 186
Libet, e7: 171
local state. *See* state, local
logic
  & negation, 123
  & propositions, 53
  & thinking, 67
  & truth, 78, 86
  & uncertainty principle, 95
  as modelling, 82
  bilogic, 85
  Birkhoff-von Neumann, 94
  context in, 86, 88, 96, 97
  distributive law, 94
  in Parmenides, 73
  in the child (Piaget), 81
  interface between knowings, 141

intuitionism, 124
logos according to
  Armstrong, 74
  negation, 84
  quantum (Chapter 4), 92
  quantum & relational, 79
  symmetric (Matte Blanco), 83
  topos, 96
  with Aristotle, 80
logos
  & *dabar* (Hebrew), 74
  & truth, 76
  & *noein*, 75
  in the *polis* (Armstrong), 74
  legein (Heidegger), 73
  Parmenides, 73
London & Bauer, 38, 101–5, 116

M
many worlds, 37
Mathews, 128, 134
Matte Blanco, 83, 85, 123
  & negation, e52: 11
  ignores types, e54: 11
  reformulation of, e50: 187
  set theory inappropriate, e51: 187
McFague, 142
McGilchrist, 24, 68, 70
  consciousness in, 70
  Homeric transition, 72
'me', 7, 11, 120
measurement, 26, 32, 92, e30: 179
  & consciousness, 36, 38
  & context, 98
  & propositions, 93
  & Zeno, 114
  apparatus, 43
  different from assertion, 124
  distinct from consciousness, 107
  for London & Bauer, 102
  measurement time, 115, 119
  photographic, 50
  pointer, 43
  propositions, 53
  Stapp's model, 116
  Stapp & conventional forms, e67: 196
  Wheeler on, 39
microtubules, 122
  & Zeno, 120
  consciousness in, 138
  quantum computing, 122
mind, *See also* Teesdale & Barnard
  & consciousness, 108
  & logic, 67
  components of, 2, 15
  dual model of, 70
  dual nature of, *See* Teasdale & Barnard
  McGilchrist on, 69
  over matter, 111
  splitting of, in quantum interpretation, 38
  systems within, 86
  various models of, 133
mixed state, 29, 39, 44, 104, 105, 106, 116. *See also* state, mixed
mixture. *See* state, mixed
modelling, 82, 113
  of Spirit, 149
  replaced by praxis, 145

N
Nagel
  what is it like to be a bat, 9, 14
  the view from nowhere, 139

nature
  choice of, 116, 123, 126, 127
  laws of, 80
negation, 53, See also logic
  details of different forms, e52: 188
  in assertion, 123
  in topos logic, 98
Newton
  & reality, 24
  concept of time, 55
  Newtonian world-view, 33
Nicholas of Cusa, coincidence of opposites, e53: 189
noein. See conceive
non-conceptuality, 18–9
notation of quantum theory, e18: 175

O

observable, quantum, 32, 41
  role of, e21: 177
observer
  as extension of apparatus, 104
  as part of cosmic Being, 140
  for Donald, 60
  in histories interpretation, 54
  in London & Bauer, 38, 101, 105
  in quantum theory, 37
  in science & consciousness, 8
  in Zeno effect, 114
  of universe, 50
  in relation to time, 51
operators, 35
orchestration
  Hameroff & Penrose, 120–3

P

Page, 60
panpsychism, 134, 158
parapsychology. See psychokinesis
Parmenides, 73, 81, 90
participatory universe, 40
Pascal, 142
Penrose, 32, 37, 122, See also Hameroff
  1-graviton collapse, e73: 198
  & consciousness, 15, 58, 107
perception, 6, 7, 17, 60
  legein, 73
  many minds interpretation, 38
phase relationship
  & uncertainty, e30: 179
Piaget, 81
Planck mass, 122
Plato, 24, 32, 77
  & Socrates, 75
Popper, 28
praxis, 150–3, 158, See also Aristotle, work
  & ethical categories, e92: 204
probability, 29, 44, 60, 62, 64, 103, 129. See also state, mixed
  & actuality, 56
  & infinite histories, e40: 185
  in history interpretation, 54
  not defined in history approach, e37: 184
  theory, history & nature of, e17: 173
projective Hilbert space,

e27: 177
proposition, 53, 94, 96, 97, 123, 124
   extended in space-time, 55
   in Matte Blanco, 85
   geometrical expression, e59: 190
propositional. *See* Teasdale & Barnard
psychokinesis, 111, 125
pure state, 44, *See also* state, mixed

Q

qabalah & Aristotle, e93: 205
qualia, 10
quantum collapse. *See* collapse interpretation
   computing, 122
quantum cosmology, 46, 139
quantum space, 31

R

Radin, 111
reality 24, 32
   & actual being, 63
   & *aletheia*, 76
   & appearance, 79
   greater than normal, 147
   hidden, 26, 64
   in itself, 64
   Kant, 7
   Kant & Eckhart, 20
   window on, 97
   & Kochen Specker, 64
recombination epoch, 48, 51
record
   & observation, 52
   & Wheeler, 40
   in The Field, 34
red shift, 46, 48
relational. *See* Teasdale & Barnard

relationship & Buber, 143
   differs from experience, 143
relativity
   & time, 51
   general, & Hartle, 57
   geometry of, 55
religion
   & GreenSpirit, 154
   concept of, 147
   sensitivity around, 146
rhetoric, 75, 80
Routley, 97, *See also* Goddard

S

Schrödinger, 31, 38
seat of consciousness. *See* consciousness, seat of
selection, 117
   approach, 60, 62
   in generalised QT, 140
   in London & Bauer, 102
   in quantum theory, 58
self
   & responsibility, 17
   implicational subsystem, 69
   'me' in Kant, 7
   meanings of, 12
   self-consciousness, 7, 11–3, 70
   social construct, 13
Self
   as object, 12
   self-consciousness in London & Bauer, 40
   self-model, 70
   self-observation, 39
   in Londond & Bauer, 102
sensation
   in consciousness, 16
   in Page, 60
   narrowness of, 63

not defining consciousness, 134
Socrates, 75, 77, 79
sophia, 150, 151
  & creation, 153
  & *qabalah*, e93: 205
soul, 5, 6
  component of person, 72
  consciousness &, 15
  in Aristotle, 150
  redundancy of, 8
space
  astronomical observation, 47
  concept of field, 35
  in Kant, 7
  Pascal's terror, 142
  quantum, 30, 31, 96
  space-time, 37
  subjective, 14
space-like
  relation in histories, 55
  relation in space-time, 51
space-time (general relativity) 57
Spinoza, 128, 156
spirit
  components of person, 5
  eye of, 132
  models of, 149
spirits in Descartes, 5
spiritual traditions, 79
splitting. *See* many worlds
Stapp, 15, 109, 114, 125
  use of Zeno, 115
  view on decoherence, e69: 197
state, 34, 36
  Hartle, 57
  local, 44, 106, 107, 112
  local, definition, e16: 172
  local, reduced from cosmos, 127
  mixed, 29, 39, 45
  of consciousness, 6, 19
  quantum, 28, 30
  wave aspect, 41
steady state theory, 47
subsystem. *See* Teasdale & Barnard

T

Teasdale & Barnard, 15, 20
  consciousness in, 20, 70
  flow between subsystems, 78
  implicational, 16
  relational & unconscious, 86
Teilhard de Chardin, 142
  Christ as universal element, e87: 203
  negative view of Cosmos, e86: 203
things
  in/for itself, 24
  what counts as a thing, 134
  which are conscious, defined, e98: 206
time
  absence of, in cosmology, e38: 185
  no first moment, e31: 180
topos logic, 90, 96
  & intuitionism, e74: 198
  windows in, 112
topos theory, 97
  what it is, e62: 194
transliminal, 148
truth, 76
  & context, 86
  & time, 88
  consistency sense, 77
  correspondence, 87
  correspondence sense, 77
  degrees of, 96
  intuitionism, 124

Newtonian, 79
revelation, 79
truth-value, 98
two-slit experiment, e29: 178

U
uncertainty
  different sorts, 27
  Heisenberg's principle, 26
  of mixed state, 45
  principles, variety of, e13: 172
  quantum, 36
unity
  & actual entities (Whitehead), 136
  & Being, 136
  in Kant, 7
  of consciousness, 11, 13
  of time in Heidegger, 61
  qualia & the self, 12
universe
  & being, 63
  as aggregate of systems, 25
  early stages of, 48
  evolution of, 47
  expansion of, 47
  participatory, 40
  quantum cosmology, 46
  splitting in Everett theory, 37
  Wheeler on early state, 51
  Wheeler's "U", 52

V
variance-covariance matrix, 45
Velmans, 10, 14, 134
viae (creation centred spirituality), 152
view from nowhere. Nagel, 139

von Neumann, 40
  formalism of measurement, e65: 195
  theory of observation, 101, 104

W
wave function, 30, 31
web of Indra, 56
  origin of story, e36: 184
what is a thing, Isham & Heidegger, e64: 195
Wheeler
  & consciousness, 40, 51
  participatory universe, 40
Whitehead
  actual entities, 136
  Divinity, 141
wholeness
  & entanglement, 138
  in definition of Being, 132
  in Kant, 13
willing
  effect of, 110
  effect on past or future event, e66: 196
  Libet on, e7: 171
  part of consciousness, 17
  psychokinesis, 111
WMAP, 48, 65
windows, quantum mechanical, e63: 194
work & Eckhart, 19, 127

Z
Zeh, 43, 45
Zeno effect, 114, *See also* assertion
Zeno time
  complications calculating, e72: 198